Power, Authority and Restrictive Practices

Alan Aldridge

Power, Authority and Restrictive Practices

A Sociological Essay on
Industrial Relations

BASIL BLACKWELL / OXFORD

**British Library Cataloguing in Publication
Data**
Aldridge, Alan
    Power, authority and restrictive practices.
    Index.
    ISBN 0-631-17230-0
    1. Title
    301.5 5   HD 8391
    Industrial relations — Great Britain

Printed and bound in Great Britain by
Billing & Sons Ltd., Guildford & London

Contents

Acknowledgements

I should like to thank Alan Fox, Anthony Heath, and above all Meryl Aldridge, for their generous help and encouragement, and for their example.

Introduction

Experts on industrial relations have allowed their work to be crippled by their own reluctance to examine seriously the work of other social scientists. The result is that the study of industrial relations badly needs an injection of theoretical argument and conceptual refinement to help make sense of data that have already been gathered, to guide future research and to inform political decisions. The need is now quite widely recognized, and the purpose of this book is to make one contribution towards meeting it. The book draws mainly on sociological work, for I believe that no discipline can do more than sociology to advance our understanding of industrial relations.

The existing literature on industrial relations in Great Britain has a hard-headed no-nonsense quality that reassures and persuades. Its authors have close links with the trade union movement and with progressive employers, and are often active on Government bodies set up to report on problems of industrial relations: so it is that the analysis and recommendations of the Royal Commission on Trade Unions and Employers' Associations (Donovan) were shaped more by academic experts on industrial relations than by any other group. Theirs, however, has been an inbred literature, the child of an over-eager division of labour. Their desire to remain in touch with the industrial world and to avoid being digested by the academic has had as its darker side a narrowness of focus and lack of ambition. For example, books are written on industrial democracy that disdain reference to the many discussions of democracy in the long history of political thought. The concept of rationality, which has puzzled philosophers, sociologists and social anthropologists is freely used in the literature of industrial relations as though its meaning were self-evident. The concept of individual and group interests suffers a similar fate. The belief that the consent of the governed gives an administration its legitimacy and creates ties of obligation in its subjects is put forward as though no social contract theorist had set pen to paper and no sociologist had discussed power and authority. It would, of course, be ridiculous to dream that the student of industrial relations should be a new Renaissance Man intimately acquainted with the intricacies and profundities of every social science: investigation has to end somewhere and human abilities are finite. Nevertheless, limited capacity is not the same thing as complacent abstemiousness.

All this is changing, gradually. Some sociologists — for example, Fox, Eldridge, and Goldthorpe — have become involved in debates about industrial relations, while industrial relations experts have turned more and more to sociology in the hope that it might give their work overall theoretical coherence or at least provide useful techniques and insights. Flanders' collaboration with Fox led to an extremely influential paper whose expressly Durkheimian stance attracted the fire of Goldthorpe and Rex. (35, 38, 81) A group of industrial relations experts have examined what they take to be the sociologist's orthodox teaching on the relationship between white-collar trade unionism and social stratification. Growing mutual interest was marked by the publication of an issue of the *British Journal of Industrial Relations* given over to the dialogue with sociology. Perhaps these beginnings are modest, but they are encouraging when seen in the context of what went before. And some marriages of sociology and industrial relations may produce offspring with the strengths of both and the weaknesses of neither.

In writing this book I should like to contribute to the dialogue. The strategy adopted is simple: to take an overworked phrase, 'restrictive practices', and examine it as closely as I can. Usually, definitions of the term are impatient affairs whose message is that we need not worry too much since we all know what we mean by it, just as we all know that the really interesting and pressing questions are: what causes restrictive practices and how can we get rid of them? Here, in contrast, my argument is that the literature which makes use of the concept of restrictive practices carries a heavy load of assumptions, many of them false, about the nature of collective bargaining and trade unionism, the rights of management, the essence of craft unions and craft consciousness, the impact of technical change, the meaning of industrial democracy, the motives lying behind the behaviour of managers and workers, the conditions under which managers can be said to have won the consent of subordinates and thus to have established the legitimacy of their rule, and the connection between the institutional arrangements through which industrial relations take place and the wider social framework in which those institutions are located. If we want to examine restrictive practices we have to face problems of this magnitude. There is no way round them, so why not force them from the shadows into the open?

In many cases 'restrictive practices' is a wild card that stands for a variety of the alleged ills of industry. To their credit, industrial relations experts have been more sensitive than most other groups to the ideological content of the concept, and when referring to it have tended to put the phrase in inverted commas or preface it with a qualifying 'so-called' in order to assert their theoretical, political and moral distance from its usual implications. Sharing their aversion to the phrase and relying greatly on their work, I hope that an open examination of 'so-called "restrictive practices" ' will help us to understand and express our own positions more clearly.

The received idea of the nature of restrictive practices is deceptively straightforward. They are union rules that prevent management from achieving the most efficient utilization of resources of men and machinery given existing technology and wage rates. To preserve the pejorative flavour of the phrase it is normally admitted that some working rules may be 'reasonable' if they shield workers against conditions that would be considered socially undesirable: these rules are transubstantiated from restrictive practices into protective safeguards.

This accepted view raises a great number of problems. Do all restrictive practices have their origin in union rules? What is their purpose? Do they have more than one purpose? Are they the result of irrational beliefs or rational calculation? Are they ever in workers' best interests? What is their effect on the firm and on society as a whole? Are they ever reasonable? What are the criteria by which we should distinguish the restrictive from the protective? Who is to decide on these criteria and on their presence or absence? How is management involved? Ought we to try to eradicate restrictive practices? If so, how are we to set about it?

An examination of the Webbs' position in *Industrial Democracy* is, I believe, a convenient introduction to the terms of the debate. The distinction they drew between two trade union philosophies, the doctrine of a living wage and the doctrine of vested interests, parallels the modern concern to separate the proper functions of trade unions from their restrictive practices. Efforts to bid up wages, to negotiate shorter hours and longer holidays and to improve the environment in which the union's members work: these were the consequences, beneficial to everybody, of following the doctrine of a living wage. Contrast these with the outcome of the doctrine of vested interests: interference in managerial decisions about the utilization of resources, including the right to hire the best workmen, the organization of work, the use of new machinery, manning standards, and the disciplining and ultimately the dismissal of workers. These harmful restrictions were justified only in rare circumstances and stemmed, the Webbs argued, from the misguided belief that workers had a right and a duty to protect their trade against what they saw as threats to it. Happily, this doctrine of vested interests and the restrictive practices to which it gave birth were fated to disappear, the Webbs predicted, because the growing pace of technical change would make restrictive practices unworkable and because the citizens of a progressive society would not tolerate shackles on efficiency. Similar hopes have been expressed, though perhaps with less conviction, in modern times. The Webbs went further, foreseeing and welcoming the decline of sectionalism in the working class and the end of a system in which labour was organized into trades — the end, literally, of trade unionism. This would imply, depending on the precise nature of the assumptions and the rigour of the logic, more flexibility in inter-union relations, or interchangeability of union cards, or industrial unionism, or finally one big union for everyone. Transcending sectional barriers within the working class meant the removal of outdated obstacles to the effective deployment and utilization of manpower. Here again similar hopes have been expressed in our own day, with industrial unionism being seen as a giant step towards the removal of restrictive practices.

The shift in trade union philosophy and tactics described by the Webbs was connected to changes in the system of social stratification and in social relations generally. These changes are, at root, those involved in the great movement, expounded by Maine, from status to contractual relations. Customs and privileges of all kinds were being swept away in the name of 'efficient citizenship'. The Webbs did not, then, treat industrial relations in isolation from wider social processes; and although their analysis can be faulted this breadth of vision is greatly in their favour.

The middle chapters of this book are taken up by a closer inspection of more modern literature on restrictive practices, a literature that usually tries to set the proper functions of unions apart from restrictive practices on the ground that the latter are an infringement of managerial rights and a bar to efficiency. The trouble is that this line of reasoning does not work, since restrictions placed on managers' freedom of action need not produce inefficiency, even if we can always be sure to recognize efficiency. In any case, efficiency is not the only thing of value in the employment relationship.

A main aim of the book is to examine the ways in which managers may be implicated in the development and continuance of restrictive practices. Are they necessarily the passive or recalcitrant victims of union power? Do they act upon beliefs about management rights or is the doctrine merely an ideology? Now, even though the doctrine of managerial rights is ideological that is not to say that it has no effect on behaviour. As with ideology so with delusions of grandeur: the man who believes himself to be Napoleon is apt to behave diffently from one who does not. When managerial rights are compromised *by people who believe in them* this will tend to produce the pattern of 'informal', haphazard and shifty dealings with shop stewards. The traditional insistence on the sanctity of managerial rights by management in the engineering industry and by the Engineering Employers' Federation has often been pointed to as one of the many causes of the weakening and frequent breakdown of agreed constitutional procedures in the sector — an unintended consequence of the doctrine of managerial rights.

Restrictive practices can be thought of as forms of deviance; and in this respect several related sociological arguments should be remembered. First, we must not draw too sharp a distinction between criminals and law-abiding citizens. There is now a good deal of evidence of the many ways in which managers at all levels are implicated in the growth and maintenance of what are usually thought to be inefficiencies. Second, we should look at the processes by which certain forms of behaviour are defined as restrictive. After all, the very phrase 'restrictive practices' is itself an historical product, since in an age when any trade union activity was held to be illegitimate it was unnecessary to speak of restrictive practices at all. Only when some ground had been lost did the phrase achieve prominence. It is not a timeless and irremovable category of thought. Third, we have to beware of assuming a consensus where none exists. Rival managerial groups, protecting and advancing their own sectional interests, are at times indistinguishable from manual workers doing the selfsame thing. Vested interests are flourishing, not only among manual workers. Indeed, one may well argue — as sociologists are increasingly coming to do — that the ancient professions themselves are built on the solid foundation of nothing other than a well-developed form of the doctrine of vested interests.

In the last two chapters I try to show that the view we take of restrictive practices is crucial in determining the kinds of industrial policy we consider desirable. Theorizing, explicit or tacit, about the nature of restrictive practices has important consequences for the behaviour of workers, management and government: there is a unity of theory and practice.

If managerial rights are being eroded what could be more sensible or more just than the use of the law to restore and uphold them? The proposal that an independent tribunal be set up to examine cases of alleged restrictive practices, to prohibit those it thought unmitigated and to penalize any firm or union failing to comply with its decisions, is discussed in Chapter Five. A number of doubts are raised about the likely success of this venture. If managers find the tribunal's judgments unpalatable they will circumvent them. On the whole managers like to preserve their autonomy and resent intervention by outside bodies, including their own associations. What is more, it would not be possible to draw up a detailed list of harmful practices since their purpose and effects can vary from one situation to another. One might envisage a law that issued a general prohibition of restrictive practices and assigned to the tribunal the job of judging every case on its merit; however, the American experience of the vague 'anti-featherbedding' clause of the Taft-Hartley Act is not encouraging. Finally, a healthy climate of industrial relations could hardly be expected to follow unpopular decisions supported by the threat of penalties. Some of the Courts of Inquiry that have been established in the past have realized just this, and have consciously chosen solutions not as the road to maximum efficiency in an ideal world but rather because they promise to create the minimum dissension possible.

The case for productivity bargaining stands in stark contrast to the legal solution. In the last chapter I am not concerned with questions about the degree to which productivity bargains may create an overall misallocation of the economy's resources, nor with the relation between the state of the economy generally and the attractiveness of productivity bargaining to managers and workers. No one could deny, however, the importance of those questions. For example, can the appeal of productivity bargaining in the 1960s be accounted for simply by the link between the Labour government's incomes policy and productivity — that is, the main way of avoiding the dead hand of income restraint was by the claim (often spurious) that pay rises were to be offset by higher productivity? Is full employment not a necessary condition of the climate in which unions will be drawn willingly into productivity deals? And how far is it true to say that productivity bargains will be especially favoured in certain types of industry — those, for instance, that are capital-intensive and that produce for very competitive international markets?

What I am concerned with is an approach to productivity bargaining that is well expressed in Flanders' classic study of the agreements at Esso's oil refinery at Fawley. Productivity agreements are seen as integral to a new kind of management and unionism, a new era of collective bargaining that McCarthy and Ellis have recently called 'management by agreement' and which, it is argued, introduces a greater degree of democracy into industry while stopping short of workers' control.

Underlying this case for productivity bargaining is a revised view of the nature of restrictive practices. For the most part they are not a matter of union rules but are arrangements that grow up at the place of work. Workers' action in enforcing restrictions is not a manifestation of blind unthinking resistance to change but is rationally based. Industrial managers at all levels are deeply involved in the growth of wasteful practices: they are largely responsible for creating the conditions in which workers respond in undesirable ways and they often turn a blind eye to or even encourage certain sorts of waste. Fortunately, the argument continues, managers are faced with a double challenge, a pincer movement from outside and from below. On the one hand, government policies and increased international competition (cartels notwithstanding) have put a financial squeeze on managers and goaded them into seeking, among other things, more efficient ways to organize work. On the other hand, the aspirations of workers have been rising. Their bargaining muscle under full employment has developed and they are demanding a bigger say on a wider range of issues. In this situation it would be futile for managers to rely on defending the citadel of managerial rights. Instead, it is argued, they are coming to see that bargaining with workers' representatives over the utilization of resources is not a profanation of the managerial mission. Thus a revision of managerial attitudes to restrictive practices (stimulated by the challenges from outside and below) is one prerequisite of successful productivity bargaining.

The revised view of restrictive practices outlined above has arisen out of a liberal, pluralist perspective on industrial relations. Strong independent trade unions are seen as an indispensable check to excessive managerial power — they are a permanent opposition party protecting the rights, freedoms and interests of subordinates in the employment relationship. Schemes of worker representation, on the other hand, are viewed with suspicion because of the danger that so-called representatives will cease to represent and become in effect managers under another guise. Trade unions, working through and extending the normal processes of collective bargaining, are the surest barrier to autocracy in industry. And provided it operates within limits set down by agreed procedural and substantive rules, industrial conflict is not bloody-minded or irrational, but is a sign that liberal democracy is healthy and vigorous.

To this dislike of managerial diktat has been added the belief — an interesting application of social contract theory — that the legitimacy of managerial authority is conferred only by the willing and active consent of the workers. Coerced obedience and sullen acquiescence are not substitutes for consent proper. Many of the problems of contemporary industrial relations are attributed to the decline of managerial authority, and productivity bargaining, with its detailed and painstaking negotiations on many aspects of employment, is seen as the means of renewing the social contract and reclaiming lost authority.

Unfortunately, pluralists have not guarded their left flank very well against attack from radicals and Marxists. For despite their repeated emphasis on the crucial role played by consent pluralists have been slow to examine the origins and character of that consent. The vital question is: is it ever possible to say that consent is the product of false consciousness? Marxists, obviously, are eager to assert that this is so: productivity deals are merely one mechanism by which capitalists forlornly hope to shore up a decaying social system, and workers who lend their support to such deals are usually acting against their own objective interests, of which they are or have been kept unaware. Part of the Marxist's duty is, therefore, to work to raise workers' consciousness, revealing to them where their objective interests lie — in the revolutionary overthrow of the capitalist order. But many pluralists, given their commitment to liberal values, think that they can do no more than take workers' wants as they stand, since to do otherwise would be an authoritarian violation of individual liberty. On this view, 'false consciousness' is the most illiberal of notions. If workers' consent is willing, these pluralists argue, then managerial legitimacy is upheld: it is not for the liberal to deny some supposedly 'objective' validity to that consent.

Between these extremes of liberalism and radicalism is a middle way — a liberalism that gives away nothing to authoritarians but is nevertheless prepared to examine the social derivation of wants and the ways in which consent can be deliberately engineered. To put the same point in another way, it is sensitive to the operation of power in determining the content of the social contract. Pluralists can use the concept of false consciousness without releasing their hold on liberal values. *Of course* it is possible that someone may be unaware of his best interests: lack of information or of foresight may lead him to act in direct opposition to his interests, as he may come to realize later. *Of course* pluralists can try to persuade this person that he is mistaken. Nothing is to stop pluralists from engaging in consciousness-raising activities — for liberals approve of open, rational debate. The point is, however, that the individual is ultimately the only judge of his interests. He has the right to disagree with outsiders' diagnoses of his situation.

If pluralists are to meet the challenge from the Left and if, moreover, they are to remain true to their liberalism, then they must be prepared to examine the origins of consent. This they can do without putting on the strait-jacket of authoritarian orthodoxies. If they are not willing to do so they will stand accused of being sophisticated apologists for the bad as well as the good in the existing social order of the West — and they may be found guilty.

One

The Webbs

Two types of unionism

First published in 1897, *Industrial Democracy* is a rich and many-sided work. It contains, as does the Webbs' earlier *History of Trade Unionism*, detailed descriptions of trade union activities; indeed, it has been said of them that they were the first social scientists to discover the British trade union movement. In addition, it offers explanations of trade union workings, ideologies and goals. It charts the development of trade unions in this country and makes predictions about their future role, predictions whose accuracy we are now able to assess. Another of their major concerns was to evaluate the economic and social contribution which unions made to the well-being not merely of their own members but also of the wider society. These four elements — description, explanation, prediction and evaluation — were all deliberately interwoven in the book.

The Webbs' view of trade unionism has made a deep impression on the study of industrial relations, particularly in this country. Their assumptions, concepts and normative judgments are often adopted, modified or challenged in contemporary studies of industrial relations, even though this influence is sometimes unrecognised or unacknowledged. Terminologies may have changed, but at a deeper level there is much that has been constant. In Flanders' influential analysis of the nature of collective bargaining there is a critical (and misleadingly incomplete) examination of the Webbs' writing on the subject. In McCarthy's detailed study of the closed shop in Great Britain — a book which, like the Webbs' work, was partly designed to fill a 'factual vacuum' and which succeeded in doing so — there are frequent references to *Industrial Democracy*. The Webbs' studies can serve as a useful introduction to the problems of industrial relations and not least to that of restrictive labour practices.

The Webbs believed that all trade union regulations could be 'reduced to two economic devices: restriction of numbers and the common rule'. (98, p. 704) The first of these was the policy of laying down strict ratios of apprentices to journeymen, a policy which aimed at pushing up wages by preventing employers from hiring too many trainees: competition for jobs would thus be contained. The device of the common rule, in contrast, represented an attempt to regulate contracts of employment throughout any given trade or industry: wage-rates must not fall below nor hours of work rise above a stipulated level, while working conditions should meet requirements of sanitation and safety. Since no attempt was made to limit competition for jobs, unions which used this device were 'open' rather than 'closed'. The distinction between the two is, for them, both clear-cut and crucial: for these are devices 'which are sharply marked off from each other, which rest on absolutely different assumptions, and which are mutually contradictory in their social results'. (98, p. Lii)

Each of these devices was associated with a system of norms and values. Whereas entry restriction was buttressed by the archaic doctrine of vested interests, which held that all those employed in a trade had a right and a duty to guard against anything which threatened the status, privilege and financial rewards of that trade, the device of the common rule received its support from the progressive doctrine of a living wage: the assertion, simply, that terms and conditions of employment should not fall below socially acceptable standards. In the third part of *Industrial Democracy*, where the theoretical examination of trade unionism coincided with the evaluation of its consequences, the Webbs were concerned above all to show that the strategy of entry restriction, unlike the enforcement of common rules, was a harmful trade union weapon but was, happily, foredoomed. So, too, the doctrine of a living wage was swiftly replacing that of vested interests.

A policy of entry restriction, they claimed, lowers productive efficiency principally by preventing the free selection of the most capable men and managers. Those already securely employed in a trade lose incentive, and managers find difficulty in establishing new plant owing to a shortage of labour. Industrial reorganization is perpetually impeded, techniques and processes become stereotyped, the productive forces of the economy are fettered. Unfortunate results of this kind were supposed not to follow from the enforcement of common rules. For whenever unions successfully demand higher wages, shorter hours and improved conditions of work, managers are obliged to look for ways of increasing productivity. Common rules are a stimulus spurring managers to respond by selecting for employment only the fittest men and by organizing their work in the most efficient manner possible. (98, pp. 705-739) In the eyes of the Webbs, managers were not an exception to Emerson's dictum that 'mankind is as lazy as it dares to be'.

This account of the reasons why the consequences of entry restriction are so different from those of the common rule has been questioned by McCarthy on two main grounds. First, is it not the case that wage rates and conditions of employment imposed by the unions may prove so costly that markets are lost and production and profits depleted, jeopardizing the competitive position of the industry in question? What ensures that common rules invariably have the beneficial effects attributed to them? Second, if an employer is stimulated by union insistence on minimum terms and conditions of employment why should his response be significantly different when he is faced with entry restriction? Any demand by a trade union is likely to add to an employer's costs, and there is no reason to suppose *a priori* that these are offset by increased efficiency only in the case of common rules. (65, pp. 194-5) This second objection could be broadened into the claim that it applies to all manner of restrictive practices besides the pre-entry closed shop. Thus Slichter and his colleagues assert: 'Perhaps the safest generalization is that make-work rules stimulate technological change. Processes will be altered so that output will no longer be restricted.' (88, p. 337)

Moreover, the objection could be strengthened by arguing that entry restriction may confer upon society as a whole specific benefits which would not necessarily follow from the enforcement of common rules. Restriction of numbers may promote labour mobility by increasing the amount of knowledge of the market or 'market transparency'. (This is, indeed, one of the many functions of trade unions: it is served, for example, by advertisements for vacancies in union journals and by the assistance given by unions to employers seeking workers who are in short supply.) Hunter, Reid, and Boddy observe that pressures from the trade union concerned have resulted in a severe limitation of the number of process engravers in the printing industry, and this, they claim, 'suggests an incidental benefit of the apprenticeship ratios operated in the industry, in that they can be used to prevent uninformed entry to the trade'. (50, p. 94) Far from impeding the march of progress for the reasons given by the Webbs, the device of restriction of numbers may on occasion ease the adjustment to technical change by dispelling fears of redundancy and solving problems of redeployment.

The Webbs were not defenceless against these objections. For one thing, they did consider the possibility that the demands embodied in common rules might be pitched uncomfortably high. This was not, they thought, a great danger, since a self-regulating mechanism would operate. If higher labour costs could not be absorbed by greater efficiency then prices would rise and demand fall, resulting in an inevitable decline in wages and a restoration of equilibrium. McCarthy acknowledges this point; but why, he asks, was there no similar mechanism to prevent the device of restriction from having its allegedly harmful effects? (65, pp. 194-5) Are not the Webbs guilty of being unjustifiably selective in their invocation of self-regulating mechanisms?

What McCarthy's argument misses is that not only did the Webbs consider entry restriction to be a harmful device, they also foresaw its disappearance from the armoury of the unions. Owing to the ever-growing mobility of labour and the incessant revolutionizing of manufacturing processes the effective use of entry restriction was already, in 1897, largely a matter of trade union history. The assertion that better working conditions may be obtained by limiting the competition for jobs 'would not be denied by any trade unionist, but it cannot be said to form an important part in the working creed of the trade union world'. (98, p. 561) Its moral and psychological underpinning, the doctrine of vested interests, was a spent force, neither motivating union leaders nor appearing in their negotiations with employers and appeals for public support. Towards the middle of the nineteenth century its place was taken by the doctrine of supply and demand (which the Webbs treat in a relatively summary fashion, mainly because they see it as a short-lived, transitional phase), and this in turn yielded before the doctrine of a living wage and the attempt to secure acceptable minimum conditions of employment throughout each trade or industry. (98, p. 595) Some working men there were who clung to the old idea of vested interests or property rights in the job; but the more progressive of their leaders had seen the need for a new rationale of union activities.

The reason for these developments is clearly stated in an important and revealing passage: 'the modern passion for progress, demanding the quickest possible adaptation of social structure to social needs, has effectually undermined the assumption that any person can have a vested interest in an occupation'. (98, p. 572) Just as the device of the common rule could not be pressed so far as to produce crippling labour costs, so too devices encouraged by the doctrine of vested interests would not be allowed to do harm in the long run. The citizens of a progressive society, fired by a passion for progress, would insist on the quickest possible adaptation of social structure to social needs. Government, entrepreneurs, consumers and workmen without such protection would not tolerate these restraints. In any case, the pace of innovation in manufacturing processes, quickened by growing international competition, was reducing the level of skill required in the crafts and undermining all attempts to establish rigid boundaries to each separate occupation. Restrictionist tactics were unworkable and the restrictionist philosophy discredited. Possibly the Webbs thought that the disappearance of the doctrine of vested interests and its associated weaponry was overdetermined.

It is not true to say, then, that the Webbs conjured up mechanisms of self-regulation selectively. On the contrary, they were vigilant in detecting them. Noxious creeds and institutions would wither while beneficial ones would flourish. Thus the desirable was happily married to the inevitable. If we agree that functionalism is best characterized as an exhortation to discover and examine self-regulating mechanisms which restore equilibrium in accordance with the system's needs and which are as prevalent in social as in biological systems, then, in *Industrial Democracy* at least, the Webbs had a functionalist orientation.

McCarthy's second objection to the Webbs' account of the consequences of common rules and entry restriction was, as explained, that one can argue that the latter device may also spur managers through the strait gate of increased efficiency. The reply to this is that the policy of restriction of numbers was conceived by the Webbs as part of a wider restrictionist strategy enshrined in the doctrine of a living wage, associated mainly with the craft unions and expressed in extreme form in the opposition to labour-saving machinery. This strategy might well 'stimulate' employers, but the difficulty was that it denied them the means necessary to the achievement of greater efficiency. Like alcohol, it provoked the desire but took away the performance. Only if trade unionism were informed by a more enlightened philosophy — one which sought its ends by the imposition of common rules — would the employer be free to introduce cost-reducing methods.

But has this new philosophy come to predominate in industrial relations? For there can be no doubt that the Webbs thought that the notion of vested interests was moribund and that the doctrine of a living wage was in the ascendant. Presumably it is not too early to assess the accuracy of their prediction. Now, if their reasoning were correct one would hardly expect that the question of vested interests or property rights would play an important role in a relatively advanced, large-scale industry such as motor vehicle manufacture. Yet a recent study of this sector revealed that the doctrine of vested interests is still a highly significant force in industrial relations. A marked change was found to have taken place in the aetiological pattern of disputes since the Second World War.

Questions of wages, above all of wage structure and work loads, retain their paramount importance; but two other areas have grown rapidly in significance, and these are the idea of fair wage comparabilities and the conviction that the performance of a job establishes property rights in it. In other countries the motor industry seems to be less prone to conflict than it is in the United Kingdom: certainly, it is less afflicted by stoppages of work. Turner and his colleagues have identified as the chief difference between British and foreign motor industries the extent to which the principles of fair wages and job property rights have been incorporated into the terms of employment. Workers in the industry in other countries have more adequate safeguards against dismissal, and both property rights and representation on the shop floor are better recognized. As evidence of this, the authors cite seniority provisions and arrangements for plant grievance settlement in the United States, and legal works councils in European countries. (96, p. 339) In Great Britain, the joint shop stewards organization, with its independence of official union bodies, has concerned itself primarily with claims to fair wages and job property rights: indeed, it was in part the failure of the official organs to deal effectively with such issues that led to the growth of the unofficial movement. (96, p. 343)

Northrup discovered a similar attachment to the doctrine of vested interests in the supermarket industry in America. Once again, if the Webbs were correct one would not have foreseen that the concept of property rights would take such a firm hold in a sector which neither appears to demand an outstanding measure of skill nor has deep historical roots in craft unionism. Yet Northrup writes that 'the concept that a particular craft of employees "owns" a particular job is well embodied in the supermarket industry, and indeed many of the restrictions might be said to come under this heading'. (78, p. 86) The 'clerks' work' clause, to cite one of the more striking examples, provides that members of the Retail Clerks International Association have the exclusive right to all work not belonging to the province of the meat department. This entails, among other things, that only in certain exceptional circumstances are vendors allowed to stock the shelves, even though this is a function that they normally perform in non-union stores.

More generally, the Contract of Employment Act of 1963 and the Redundancy Payments Act of 1965 included recognition of job ownership and some provision for compensation for loss of employment, financed by the employer. The doctrine of vested interests, which the Webbs thought obsolescent, has thus been accorded a degree of legal support.

Craft unions and craft consciousness
In order to understand both the basis of the Webbs' predictions and the reasons for their inaccuracy it may be useful to begin by looking at some features of craft unionism: for where, if not in the craft unions, shall we find at their most developed the device of restriction of numbers and the doctrine of vested interests? The Webbs considered that apprenticeship ratios and the exclusion of 'illegal men' had been crucial to the unionism of the eighteenth century, but that these were passing phenomena. The perpetual revolutionizing of technology was creating conditions in which the boundaries between jobs were always shifting and the 'skill gap' between journeymen, assistants and labourers was progressively narrowing, thereby undermining claims to property rights in the job. Since these fluid conditions were precisely what characterized all that was modern in industry, entry restriction and vested interests could not long survive.

However, although it can be argued that the narrowing of a skill gap will be likely to encourage semi-skilled assistants and unskilled labourers to lay claim to the work performed by the skilled group, and even though they will be successful in many cases, it is still possible for boundaries to be redrawn so as to create a new skill gap. And although a new set of property lines may be strongly resisted at first, they can be defended in their turn as staunchly as the old. For instance, in response to the development of linotype and monotype composing machines towards the end of the last century, the Typographical Association was compelled to admit many new men who had not served an apprenticeship. Once admitted, however, these men joined the time-served craftsmen in resisting any encroachment on the new skilled domain. Therefore, as

McCarthy notes, the Typographical Association was able to combine intermittent use of an 'open door' policy with the long-term pursuit of entry control and craft status. (65, p. 138) This is not to deny that the printing unions were fortunate in at least two respects: the mechanical innovations arrived at a time when the demand for the printed word was increasing rapidly, and the three main machines (the Hattersley, the Linotype and the Monotype) followed each other by about a decade, thus giving the unions a chance to work out their strategy. (16, pp. 165-183) If the historical conditions had been less favourable the unions would have been faced with a harder battle — one which they might have lost. But they did not lose. The victory of the 'imperatives' of technical change is not, then, guaranteed. Recalling the point made earlier about the functionalist approach implicit in the Webbs' analysis, it must be said that even if we can make sense of the concept of 'social needs' and even if we can be sure that we have identified them correctly, it still does not follow that social structures will 'adapt' to these needs as quickly as possible. The impact of a printing machine on a social system is less calculable than its impact on a piece of paper.

The attitude of union leaders at this crucial time in the history of printing has been well characterized by Child: 'If pragmatism is a virtue then the union leaders were virtuous men. They established their "principles", but they knew when to turn a blind eye to an irremediable breach. They modified their rules, educated their members, bargained with the employers, gave way when the opposition was too strong. Thus the unions emerged unscathed from the process. Neither the TA nor the LSC (the London Society of Compositors) suffered even a temporary set-back in the growth of membership. Even the added financial burden of the extra unemployed hardly affected their funds.' (16, p.182)

The error of the Webbs' prediction derives largely from their misconception of the nature of a skill gap and the correlative problem of what actually constitutes a craft. Technical developments were dissolving the skill gap; *ergo,* craft status and craft privilege would wither away. They saw skill as something which could be defined objectively, that is, it could be discerned and measured by interpersonally verifiable techniques. One might measure it, for example, by determining the amount and length of training necessary to the performance of a number of tasks, concluding that only those which demanded long and intensive training should be considered to be skilled.

Some such procedure was clearly what the authors of *Industrial Democracy* had in mind; but it is shot through the difficulties. Since these difficulties are analogous to those encountered when attempts are made to measure 'professionalism' a fuller treatment of them will be deferred until a later chapter dealing with the professions. The point to be made here is that the Webbs' account of craft unionism treats craft consciousness as a mere epiphenomenon of objectively measured job requirements: the socio-psychological dimension is not considered to be an independent factor in a causal explanation of the development and eventual dissolution of craft unionism.

The objection to the Webbs' portrait of craft unionism could take either a strong or a weak form. In the strong version, it makes no sense to seek objective measurements of skill. Skill is one element in a socially constructed reality, and has no meaning apart from that social construction. If the relevant groups define an occupation as skilled then it *is* skilled: that is all there is (and could be) to it. Skill gaps exist if and only if they are thought to exist. How, for example, are we to determine the amount of training *necessary* to the *adequate* performance of a job? Where are our criteria of necessity and adequacy? Although we can readily discover how long an apprenticeship is stipulated by the trade union concerned, this completely avoids the issue. Nor will it do simply to ask employers how long a period of training they consider sufficient. Thus the man who claims that a task is not really skilled or is more skilled than has been supposed simply makes a bid to enter the negotiation of our social reality. His talk of objective measurement is quite spurious. It is no more than a weapon he uses to win the power-holders over to his own interpretation.

This does not rule out any examination of the historical situations in which a group will be likely to succeed in an effort to establish or retain its identity as a craft. Child's discussion of the reasons why unions in the printing industry were able to assimilate technical changes at the end of the last century is perfectly compatible with the position outlined. We should simply say that the buoyant demand for the industry's product together with the gradualness of the introduction of new machinery made it easier for the unions to preserve their craft status.

Industrial sociologists and industrial relations experts have tended to shy away from the strong objection and have adopted a weaker version — weaker not in the sense that it is less valid but merely that it makes a less extensive claim. It is admitted that there can be objective measurements of skill but denied that skill is a necessary condition of craft unionism. While it may well be true to say that the more technical competence a group of workers possesses the more inclined and the better able it will be to adopt those attitudes and that organization which characterize the crafts, it does not follow that craft unionism is invariably based on a highly skilled work force. Most or all of the specific features of craft unionism — identification with an occupational community, pride in the job, a professed concern for work of good quality, a distinctive body of tradition and culture, relatively egalitarian authority relations, strict observance of lines of demarcation, a tendency to demand exclusive jurisdiction over new processes and an independent approach to collective bargaining — may exist alongside an attenuated skill gap. They will not necessarily disappear, even in the long run.

In his study of unions in the cotton trade Turner argues that few jobs in this sector can be called skilled if skill is taken to imply that their performance requires long and rigorous training. Nor are there any arresting differences in the competence demanded by the various occupations which make up the trade. (94, pp. 110-111) Nevertheless, distinctions of skill are drawn. The salient point is that 'many "skills" are actually the product of trade unionism itself, instead of *vice versa*'. (94, p. 194) This is surely true of most sectors of industry.

The argument has been pushed one stage further by hypothesizing that the more notional a skill gap becomes the greater is the significance of craftsmanship in the eyes of the soi-disant craftsmen. (30, p. 216) Far from demolishing craft consciousness, technical progress may reinforce it. Flanders' study of the productivity agreements at Fawley, for example, showed that welders formed one of the main centres of resistance to proposals for inter-craft flexibility. They insisted that their status as craftsmen be maintained. But welding does not enjoy an established prestige and varies widely in the degree of expertise it demands. Often, welders are regarded as little more than semi-skilled operatives and are organized by a general rather than a craft union. Welding occupies a marginal position in the organization of work and other craftsmen frequently display competence in it. Threatened with a loss of status the welders at Fawley responded by insisting more vociferously than many of the other work groups in the plant on their own privileges. Their protests were successful. The fact, then, that a skill gap has become more tenuous in terms of the abilities it calls forth does not mean that the craft preserve will necessarily be eroded.

For a further example of the phenomenon of craft resistance to the 'imperatives' of technical change we may turn again to the printing industry, and specifically to the workers organized by the Society of Lithographic Artists, Designers, Engravers and Process Workers (SLADE). Representatives of the International Publishing Corporation made it very clear in their oral evidence before the Donovan Commission that they considered SLADE to be the most obstructive of the unions with which they had to deal. (52, p. 2,627) In particular, they objected to the union's 'white card' policy, under which any employer who had a vacancy calling for a member of SLADE had to apply to the union, which would then send an applicant. No one denied that the employer retained the freedom to reject any applicant; nevertheless, the white card policy was an irritant since it was an infringement of the managerial right of hiring and firing and was a symptom of the union's strict entry restriction.

It is not hard to discover the pressures acting on SLADE and its members. Declining job opportunities are aggravated by technical changes in printing processes which besides lessening the demand for their work have also reduced the amount of skill required for its performance. (50, pp. 70-2) Powderless etching, in particular, needs far less labour and is appreciably faster than the conventional technique of engraving; it is also simpler.

Given this background of declining opportunities for employment and threats to the craft status of its members, one can see why SLADE should insist on entry restriction and other guarantees against redundancy, and why process engravers should stand out for the maintenance of their privileged position. Their situation is similar to that of the welders at Fawley. It is not surprising that the firm of efficiency consultants which submitted a report to the Royal Commission on the Press found that: 'In general, the greater the skill or craft involved the less is the excess staffing — and conversely, the biggest excuses are usually found in those departments and unions where the skill required is least.' (85, p. 210)

Flanders' hypothesis (that craft consciousness tends to be heightened when a skill gap becomes more notional) can be reformulated to fit in with the strong critique of the Webbs' position. Skill gaps narrow when managers and other groups of workers begin to withdraw legitimacy from the claim that the group in question possesses a body of expertise. In this situation, it is suggested, the group's self-consciousness will be increased and it will fight hard to uphold the integrity of its position. Just as the experience of persecution (real or imagined) can augment the vitality and exclusiveness of a religious sect, so the unfavourable reactions of others may have a similar effect on a craft union.

The conclusion is, therefore, that any definition of craft unionism which is based solely on notions of technical competence and training cannot do justice to the reality of the crafts as social organizations. Craft consciousness is more than a mere by-product of job specifications. Nor does technical change have an automatic impact on social arrangements. From false premises the Webbs deduced a false conclusion.

Trade unions and sectionalism

In his discussion of the nature of collective bargaining, Flanders asks the question, what is the basis of the distinction between restriction of numbers and the common rule? For every regulation, whatever its source, may be said to restrict entry to an occupation. It is inherent in any rule — whether imposed by law or public custom, by employer or trade union — that its enforcement excludes all who cannot or will not abide by it. This applies to all rules, including 'common' ones. Conversely, restriction of numbers was itself a common rule, since it was the practice of enforcing apprenticeship ratios throughout a trade. Common rules may restrict numbers, and restriction of numbers is a common rule. Why, then, did the Webbs draw a distinction between the two devices? Why did they include under the device of the common rule only 'the more modern rules directly fixing a standard rate, a normal day, and definite conditions of sanitation and safety'? (98, p. 704)

'The real basis of their distinction', Flanders replies, 'Was between the market or economic processes that trade unions were seeking to control. What they were calling the device of the common rule, by fixing a minimum or uniform price for labour or settling other standard terms or conditions of employment, was in effect directly regulating *bargaining* in labour markets. The device of the restriction of numbers, on the other hand, was directly regulating *competition* by restricting the supply of labour or its demand.' (31, p. 4) As it stands this answer is surely incomplete. The *prize* of the competition which the device of restriction of numbers regulates is *'the trade'*. The doctrine of vested interests gives rise to and legitimates a whole range of devices whose main purpose is to protect the trade against perceived threats of all kinds.

When they are explaining what they mean by restriction of numbers the Webbs say that it comprises 'the ancient trade union prescriptions as to apprenticeship, the exclusion of new competitors from a trade, and the assertion of a vested interest in a particular occupation'. (98, p. 704) Here three items are jumbled. Apprenticeship ratios are one means of limiting competition for jobs: several other provisions, for example seniority rules, have the same effect. And, of course, the system of apprenticeship serves other ends as well: most notably, it is a powerful agency for the socialization of young trainees into the customs and traditions of the trade and the union. Finally, the assertion that a worker has a vested interest in an occupation is on a different plane altogether. It is not a device. It is a normative statement supplying the psychological impetus behind and ethical justification of a battery of restrictionist tactics, of which apprenticeship ratios are but one.

This last point emerges in many passages in *Industrial Democracy*. Thus: 'By the doctrine of vested interests we mean the assumption that the wages and other conditions of employment hitherto enjoyed by any section of workmen ought under no circumstances to be interfered with for the worse. It was this doctrine, as we have seen, which inspired the long struggle, lasting down to about 1860, against the introduction of machinery, or any innovation in processes. It is this doctrine which today gives the bitterness to demarcation disputes, and lies at the back of all the regulations dealing with the "right to a trade". It does more than anything else to keep alive the idea of "patrimony" and the practice of a lengthened period of apprenticeship, whilst it induces the workmen of particular trades to cling fondly to the expedient of limiting the numbers entering those trades, even after experience has proved such a limitation to be impracticable. But the doctrine of vested interests extends much further than these particular regulations. There is scarcely an industry in which it will not be found, on one occasion or another, inspiring the defence of the customary rates of wages or any threatened privilege. In some cases, indeed, we find the whole argument for trade unionism based on this one conception.' (98, pp. 562-3) As an example of the articulation of this doctrine by trade unionists themselves they cite the Birmingham Wireworkers, who proclaimed: 'Considering that the trade by which we live is our property, bought by certain years of servitude, which gives to us a vested right, and that we have a sole and exclusive claim on it, as all will have hereafter who purchase it by the same means. Such being the case, it is evident it is our duty to protect, by all fair and legal means, the property by which we live, being always equally careful not to trespass on the rights of others.' (98, p. 564)

Adherence to the notion of vested interests involved not simply apprenticeship ratios but also demarcation disputes, the fight against new machines, and hostility towards any development which put the standing of the trade in question. Summarizing their achievement in *Industrial Democracy* the Webbs said: 'we demonstrated that the regulations based on the device of restriction — *whether of numbers or output, whether in the use of machinery or in transformation of processes* — were wholly injurious not only to the trade concerned and to the community as a whole, but also to the manual worker himself.' (98, p. Lii, emphasis added) In modern terms, these are restrictive practices. They are an attempt to regulate 'managerial' relations. Managerial relations cover what management does with the labour it has hired, and this embraces the functions of recruitment, training, deployment, organization, discipline and dismissal of workers. In contrast, the doctrine of a living wage encouraged intervention only in 'market' relations, which are concerned with the terms and conditions on which labour is hired, i.e. the provisions in the contract of employment concerning wage rates, hours of work, holiday arrangements and the like.

Although the distinction between managerial and market relations is important, the terminology may mislead. For one cannot simply assume that market relations are completely determined by the impersonal workings of supply and demand; nor should one beg the question by taking it for granted that managerial relations are or ought to be laid down by management alone. Both managerial and market relations may be established by managers and workers acting in concert: both may rest on a basis of common decision-making. To allow for this possibility, it is better to formulate the distinction in terms of norms entering into the contract of employment ('contract norms') and norms governing the utilization of labour and other resources ('utilization norms'). (33, p. 158)

The doctrine of a living wage held that unions ought to engage in a struggle for better terms and conditions of employment for their members. If the details of the employment contract were left to be shaped solely by market forces this would often result in very low wages, exhausting hours and intolerable working conditions. (98, p. 712) The enforcement of common rules would act directly to prevent this. In complete contrast, the doctrine of vested interests justified workers' attempts to establish norms governing the utilization of resources. If decisions taken in this area menaced the trade, its status and rewards, then workers ought to resist them. Too much competition for jobs could be forestalled by the apprenticeship system; trespass by rival trades would cause demarcation disputes; harmful innovations by management itself might well bring trouble. Under the living wage philosophy trade unions exercised their 'proper' functions; when fed on notions of vested interests and property rights they spawned restrictive practices.

By focussing on the clash between the doctrine of vested interests and that of a living wage, rather than on the difference between restriction of numbers and the common rule, it becomes clear that at the heart of ideas of vested interests is the view that the trade must be protected. A union movement informed by such a perspective would be divided into discrete groups, each jealously guarding its own petty preserve against trespass. Little would be done to advance interests common to most working men: rewards and benefits would be won by strong unions largely at the expense of the weak. When every group promotes only those interests which it has as a group, interests shared by all are neglected. As the Webbs noted: 'Trade unionists are, for instance, unanimously in favour of drastic legislation to put down "sweating" in all trades whatsoever. But no salaried officer of the trade union world feels it to be his business to improve the Labour Code for any industry but his own. Thus, whereas the Factory Acts have been effectively elaborated to meet the special circumstances of a few trades, for all the rest they remain in the form of merely general prohibitions which it is practically impossible to enforce.' (99, pp. 477-8)

Towards the end of their history of trade unionism the Webbs addressed this problem of sectionalism. True, they were able to discern in the union movement's history an instinctive solidarity, a profound belief in the brotherhood of labour which inspired mutual aid between trades and short-lived attempts to form general unions. Nevertheless, 'the basis of the association of these million and a half wage-earners is, primarily, sectional in nature. They come together, and contribute their pence, for the defence of their interests as boilermakers, miners, cotton-spinners, and not directly for the advancement of the whole working class. Among the salaried officers of the unions, it is, as we have said, the trade official, chosen and paid for the express purpose of maintaining the interests of his own particular trade, who is the active force. *The effect has been to intensify the sectionalism to which an organization based on trades must necessarily be prone.* The vague general collectivism of the non-commissioned officers has hitherto got translated into practical proposals only in so far as it can be expressed in projects for the advantage of a particular trade.' (99, p. 477) The point had been reached where the urgent need was not to boost the earnings of the better paid, well-organized section of the working class but rather to raise the standard of living of those below the poverty line. (98, p. xl)

There was hope for the future. As unions matured there was an 'increased sense of solidarity among all sections of wage-earners', a 'widening of sympathies and strengthening of bonds of fellowship', a 'widening of the mental horizon, a genuine elevation of the trade union movement'. (99, p. 408) All this was shown by the greater willingness to recruit women, the establishment of local joint committees of rival societies, the formation of larger federations, and growing participation in international socialist congresses. The transcending of sectionalism corresponded, of course, to the transition to the new era of the doctrine of a living wage. It was their aim in *Industrial Democracy* to prove the desirability and inevitability of the process.

Two reasons are given for regarding the doctrine of restriction as unacceptable. First, it leads to the ossification of the existing industrial order; second, it produces the moral evil of in-groups clinging to their advantageous position and preventing outsiders from trying to share the benefits with them. Common rules do neither.

Now, when they are discussing common rules the Webbs sometimes say that these are enforced throughout a trade and sometimes that they apply to a whole industry. There are serious and familiar problems, which they do not tackle, of defining the boundaries of trades and industries. What is

more, the two terms are hardly synonymous. To speak of
trades is to place emphasis on workers' definitions of the
situation and on the accidents of history. To speak of
industries directs our attention to definitions imposed on the
situation from outside.

Their arguments against the transient doctrine of supply
and demand (with its corresponding feature, sliding scales)
show that they believe that common rules must be at least
factory-wide. The limitation of sliding scales was illustrated by
the impossibility of adjusting 'the ventilation, drainage,
temperature, sanitary conveniences, and safety of a cotton-
mill or engineering establishment, in proportion to the eight or
ten different sections of workpeople there employed'. (98, p.
583) But if the doctrine of a living wage means the imposition
of common rules throughout a trade then the same objection
holds, since there is likely to be more than one trade in any
establishment. Common rules would then have the same
drawback as sliding scales. With each trade union trying to
enforce its own standards the overall result would be
haphazard.

If what the Webbs had in mind was that common rules
would apply not to trades but throughout industries, this
would surely imply that labour ought to be organized in
industrial unions. Under the new dispensation union activities
would be confined to the struggle for higher wages, shorter
hours and better conditions — and what warrant does this give
for the existence of more than one union in an industry? Since
the concept of a trade is derived from the doctrine of vested
interests, the passing of that doctrine brings with it the demise
of *trade* unions. This point seldom rises to the surface in their
work — perhaps it is most clearly seen in their strictures on
sectionalism in the *History* — but it is implicit in their
argument.

Once this line of reasoning takes off it is hard to stop it. For
a commonplace in discussions of industrial unionism is that it
is impossible to draw any better than rough and ready (and
ultimately arbitrary) divisions between different industries,
especially in the light of rapid technological change.
Furthermore, as the Donovan Commission observed when it
examined the case for industrial unionism, such a union in an

ailing industry must decline along with that industry. But unions are organizations which develop organizational interests. They will fight for those interests, and this may well mean the re-emergence of restrictionist tactics. The logic of the argument may lead us not to stop at industrial unionism but to envisage the ultimate unification of labour into one big union.

The aspiration for one big union was nurtured in most of the general unions which developed towards the end of the nineteenth century. Interchangeability of union cards ('one man, one ticket') was seen as a move in the right direction. However, as Hobsbawm points out, it was not long before the local job monopoly — the policy of 'one ticket, one job' — reasserted itself. Instead of adding to the unions' power immigrant workers were presumptively blacklegs. Union leaders voiced the fear that employers would deliberately attract a surplus of labour in order to weaken the bargaining position of the more stable and loyal unionists. Unimpeded labour mobility was an attack on union interests. The 'new unionism' came to resemble the old. (48, 189-191) Whether the new leaders of labour were inspired by the doctrine of a living wage and demanded, together with their progessive fellow-citizens, the removal of all barriers to mobility and of all restraints to the adaptation of social structures to social needs; or whether they were revolutionaries who saw that the restrictionist philosophy divided the labour movement into fragments each of which possessed a merely trade union consciousness and sought its limited objectives by merely reformist tactics, the upshot was that sectionalism prevailed.

In its discussion of industrial unionism the Donovan Commission foresaw several disadvantages to such a system. It is hard to draw boundaries between different industries, especially in the light of rapid technological change; sectional claims can arise in industrial unions as in any organization; craft unions, founded on trades rather than on industries, may in some cases be better at encouraging labour mobility; it may be hard to organize white-collar workers on industrial lines; when industries decline unions will fight to avoid dying with them; industrial unionism does not provide a guarantee against unconstitutional shop floor action divorced from formal union control; nor would it be possible, given the current arrangement of industrial relations in Great Britain, to usher in the new order without serious upheavals. (24, pp. 179-86) But just as interchangeability of union cards could be an acceptable substitute for the ideal of one big union, so the Commission thought that the benefits of industrial unionism could be won by more modest reforms. Inter-union agreements on negotiating and recruiting rights, in particular, would be a giant step. Even here, the interests of the various unions would have to be protected: 'The success of the agreement would, of course, depend on matching losses and gains for each union.' (24, p. 182) Such a statement shows the tribute which the system of industrial relations pays to the doctrine of vested interests.

Unions and social change

Unlike much of the work of later writers *Industrial Democracy* is more than a study of industrial relations as a relatively self-contained system. The envisaged transformation of trade union methods and of the rationale of union activities mirrored structural changes which were taking place in the wider society. The passing of the trades and of craft consciousness marked the end of sectionalism and the birth of unity and solidarity in the working class. The newer unionism was thus bound up with changes in the system of social stratification in modern industrial societies.

When we turn to sociological studies of stratification we find that the picture painted by the Webbs is more abstract than representational. Among Marxist thinkers it is precisely the *lack* of a unified class consciousness among workers that is an overriding problem of theory (and practice) ; and whether this lack is explained, for example, by the temporary ability of imperialist regimes to support themselves on the ruthless exploitation of foreign labour, or by a bourgeois cultural hegemony which implants, through mass communications, 'false' needs for material comfort, the fact is that the proletarians, called upon to unite in the overthrow of their oppressors, have been disappointing. However, Marxists have been able for some years to discern the gradual reduction of social differentiation among the working class; and they claim that it is this dynamic tendency which bourgeois sociologists neglect.

Many of these latter have emphasised that detailed investigations of different occupations are necessary to any adequate treatment of the broader questions of social stratification. As Cannon has said: 'For certain purposes the concept of "class" is too crude for analysis: the term "skilled working class", for example, is used far too loosely as if it were a homogeneous category. A further stage in the study of stratification may well be the development of typologies of occupations; in the formulation of such typologies the nature and influence of the working group are likely to be prominent factors.' (14, p. 183) This theme has often formed a part of a critique of Marxist writings on class consciousness. Thus Goldthorpe argues that 'to speak of different modes of consciousness as being "true" or "false" would seem rather obviously unsatisfactory where these can be related to systematic differences *within* the working class (as defined in Marxist terms) which may in turn be associated with the differential location of occupational or other groups in the structure of market, work and community relationships'. (39, p. 354) He refers us to Lockwood's work on the sources of variation in working class images of society. (61)

Studies of particular occupational and work groups have tended to underscore Cannon's point that the concepts which are normally used in the analysis of social stratification presuppose more unity and homogeneity than actually exist in the societies under scrutiny. Brown and Brannen's work on Tyneside shipbuilders revealed the craftsmen's sense of exclusiveness, their fidelity to the trade and their wish to secure it against encroachments by the unskilled and semi-skilled: all this made the likelihood of common action slight. (10) Wedderburn and Crompton came to similar conclusions about the relations between skilled workers and the rest. (100) Nor, as Goldthorpe argues, are there compelling reasons for supposing that the future will be very different. However spectacular the growth of white-collar unions in this country may have been, there is reason to doubt that this shows clerical workers' increasing sense of solidarity with their manual counterparts — on the contrary, the industrial militancy of white-collar workers often derives from a sense of relative deprivation and a desire to restore differentials in pay, conditions and style of life. As for those industries which are the advance guard of technical change (and therefore, presumably, harbingers of the future), these seem capable of embracing a wide variety of attitudes and behaviour among the workers who man them. On the basis of such evidence and in contrast to the kind of society foreshadowed in *Industrial Democracy*, Goldthorpe's scenario is that we are witnessing 'the splitting apart of the working class into, on the one hand, a relatively affluent and secure section, comprising the better-organized occupational groups, and, on the other, an "underclass" incorporating not only the unemployed, the unemployable and the disreputable but also the mass of unorganized unskilled workers and, most significantly, of immigrant labour exposed to derogation and discrimination on an ethnic or racial basis'. (39, p. 357) Even here, the claim is not being made that there is growing social homogeneity within each of these two groupings.

Thus the transition from the doctrine of vested interests to the doctrine of a living wage implied greater changes than mere tinkering with the system of industrial relations. It involved and reflected a change in the whole character of society, one akin to the development of 'progressive' societies, expounded by Sir Henry Maine, from relations founded on status to contractual relations. 'Starting, as from one terminus of history, from a condition of society in which all the relations of persons are summed up in the relations of family, we seem to have steadily moved towards a phase of social order in which all these relations arise from the free agreement of individuals.' (69, pp. 140-1) Maine's *Ancient Law* described and accounted for this process. The attraction of freedom of contract was that it was seen to provide a means of abolishing a body of archaic institutions which hindered the harmonious development of society. (23, p. 151) Upholding the principle of freedom of contract was part of the Benthamite, individualist struggle against any restriction of human liberty which could not be justified on utilitarian grounds. Each person, with the possible exception of children and the insane, was deemed to be the best judge of his own happiness; hence, no unnecessary constraints ought to be put on the pursuit of individual happiness.

One consequence of this was the need for freedom of movement: 'As against a legal status determined by ties and conditions outside personal decisions, contract allows the individual to change his country or employment.' (36, p. 89) Relations based on status, on the other hand, tended to limit freedom of movement and restrict competition for employment. There can be no doubt where the allegiance of the authors of *Industrial Democracy* lay as between these two states of society. Of the doctrine of a living wage they wrote: 'It is quite consistent with the freedom of every wage-earner to choose or change his occupation, and with the employer's freedom to take on whichever man he feels best fitted for his work. Thus it in no way checks mobility or stops competition.' (98, p. 590) Entry restriction and other stratagems engendered by the doctrine of vested interests were a denial of these freedoms.

But what are we to say if power is unequally divided between the parties to a contract? What of the gulf between the formal equality of parties freely to conclude contracts and the actual inequality caused by differences in bargaining power? One answer is, of course, that the weaker should combine to improve their position. The debate over the right of combination split the liberal camp in half. The Webbs' line was clear: they recognized that where bargaining power is unequal the stronger party is free to dictate terms to the weaker, and the latter is free to knuckle under. With individual bargaining the particular exigencies of particular workers could be so manipulated as to force down wages and keep other conditions of employment at a socially unacceptable standard. Indigent workers could be compelled to suffer low wages and an insanitary, unsafe working environment; similarly, the exceptional performance of 'ox-like men' would ruin piece rates for the average worker. Through collective bargaining — the presentation of collective demands to the employer by a united work force — labour could avoid the exploitation by a *tertius gaudens* of its own internal differences and divisions.

The Webbs were prepared, then, to accept combination as a means of equalizing power: collective bargaining would be fairer than individual bargaining. Obviously enough, collective bargaining assumes collective organization; yet, curiously, the Webbs were insensitive to the workings of trade unions *as organizations,* an insensitivity that showed most conspicuously when they described the coming unionism based on the doctrine of a living wage. The need to recruit, retain and discipline members — with all the problems, the exclusiveness, the obligations and rights that the notion of membership implies — is passed over lightly in *Industrial Democracy.* Similarly, they ignored conflicts of interest with rival trade unions and with non-unionists — for many of these conflicts were thought to be the outcome of the moribund doctrine of vested interests. Perhaps, as argued earlier, they nurtured the hope that eventually there would be one big union for all workers, free from any internal clashes of vested interest. Whether or not this is so, it remains true that they did not face up to the problems of collectivism and its relation to the freedom of the individual.

Two

Managerial Rights

The distinction between utilization and contract norms, between managerial and market relations, is central to an understanding of what is meant by restrictive practices. For these practices are normally so defined that they include only attempts by a trade union to regulate the area of managerial relations. This is shown clearly in the definition given by Weinstein. Adopting the tendentious American terminology he writes that 'featherbedding is defined as a labour working rule which causes the firm to hire more labour units of a particular type than it would at the existing wage, assuming technology and social norms to be given'. (101, p. 45) Hartman, too, offers a similar formulation. (44, p. 42) To take wages as given may imply that unions are free to try to influence market relations by pressing for more favourable terms and conditions of employment: nowhere does Weinstein say that a union attempt to bid up wages is illegitimate. There are, of course, many economists who argue that the unions cannot succeed even in this, since the proportion of the gross national product paid out to labour in the form of wages is a constant determined solely by laws inherent in the market system. But this is a rather different point, for a futile endeavour is not necessarily to be condemned.

The notion that unions should not be allowed to trespass on the area of managerial relations by establishing norms governing the utilization of resources, constitutes the modern doctrine of managerial rights. In the past, more sweeping claims were made on behalf of management. Thus G. F. Baer, President of the Philadelphia and Reading Railroad, declared in 1902: 'The rights and interests of the labouring man will be protected and cared for — not by the labour agitators, but by the Christian men to whom God in his infinite wisdom has given the control of the property interests of the country, and upon the management of which so much depends.' (1, p. 187) This was a theory of management by divine right; it was also an undifferentiated view, in that no attempt was made to specify which areas of decision-making were sacrosanct and which others could justifiably be subject to regulation by unions. Since all issues were to be decided by management there was no place for a rival structure of power and authority in the industrial system. The very existence of trade unions was a violation of managerial prerogative.

Taylorism

At first glance it may seem that the founder of the school of 'Scientific Management', F. W. Taylor, was of this opinion. His aversion to trade unions was famed and undisguised. It was his belief that unionism implied a general lowering of wages in order merely to bolster the earnings of the incompetent, the indolent and the inebriate. Of himself he writes: 'He is firmly convinced that the best interests of workmen and their employers are the same; so that in his criticism of labour unions he feels that he is advocating the interests of both sides.' (90, p. 185) In spite of this it is possible to detect in the Taylorite approach to the problems of industry a more modern version of the doctrine of managerial rights, incorporating the distinction between managerial and market relations and a limited view of the proper functions of trade unions.

Taylor was quite convinced that there was 'one best way' of performing any operation and that it was discoverable by what he rashly took to be scientific techniques. Since only managers had both the motive and the intelligence to discover the one best way in each case, the planning of production should be in their hands alone. At the core of his approach was a belief in the need for managers to reassert their control over production: under the traditional type of unscientific management most establishments were 'really run by the workmen, not by the bosses'. (91, pp. 48-9) The techniques of his own system — the breaking down of each operation into its component parts, which were each timed on a stop-watch — made it possible for the first time for managers to determine objectively what constituted a fair day's work. Having discovered this, management had sole responsibility for imposing the new organization of production: 'It is only through *enforced* standardization of methods, *enforced* adoption of the best implements and working conditions, and *enforced* co-operation that this faster work can be assured. And the duty of enforcing the adoption of standards and of enforcing this co-operation rests with the *management* alone.' (91, p. 83) The part of the worker was to obey. 'Schmidt' (Taylor's inspired pseudonym for a Dutch immigrant) was informed that 'a high-priced man has to do exactly as he's told from morning till night'. (91, p. 45) Selection, training, organization, deployment, discipline: all were key elements in Taylor's system, and all should be the responsibility of management.

The question of wages, on the other hand, received far less detailed attention from Taylor; in fact, he fudged the issue. He did, indeed, make it very clear that the *method* of remuneration ought always to be individual piecework: since personal ambition was the strongest force motivating men to give their best efforts, to herd them into gangs would only stunt their initiative. Again, managers are counselled not to provide too rapid and too large an increase in their workers' earnings, for while a substantial rise in income would encourage thrift, deferred gratification, sobriety and steadiness of application to the job, an immoderate rise would foster irregularity, shiftlessness, extravagance and dissipation. But what is an immoderate rise in income, and what should the level of wages under Scientific Management eventually be? The only reply Taylor could give was that Scientific Management would provide a 'special incentive', i.e. a wage that was high in relation to the worker's previous level of earnings and to the average for his trade. Not only is this answer vague, it also creates a serious problem for the whole Taylorite approach. The implication is that whereas the 'one best way' of performing each operation was determined uniquely by invariant properties of the human organism and of physical materials, the optimum level of wages was a product of the worker's past experiences, reference groups, aspirations and values. The process of unearthing the best way of performing a task is very different from the way in which we should hit upon a proper wage. In the former endeavour, on Taylor's account, we see man as a biological machine, while in the latter we treat him as a social being. If this is so, then may not the unions play a useful part in stimulating a revolution of rising expectations? Can they not aim at widening workers' horizons, encouraging them to demand more from life and persuading their employers to take a more generous view of what is socially acceptable and desirable?

Taylor saw the force of the question. When a Congressional committee was set up to investigate the working of his system he testified that his objection to unions was aimed against their practice of output restriction. He professed to share their goals of higher wages and shorter hours of work. He even went so far as to write that: 'The labour unions — particularly the trades unions of England — have rendered a great service, not only to their members, but to the world, in shortening the hours of labour and in modifying the hardships and improving the conditions of wage workers.' (90, p. 186)

To make sense of this, to reconcile it with Taylor's outright condemnation of unions, it is important to see that his teaching was largely prescriptive: he sought to change the world as well as to understand it. Rather than simply undertaking an analysis of current practice in industrial relations he pointed the way to the new era that could be ushered in by embracing the philosophy and the techniques of Scientific Management. His denunciation of union activities should therefore be interpreted as an assertion that they would be unnecessary and harmful under a system of Scientific Management. 'Soldiering will cease', he proclaimed, 'because the object for soldiering will no longer exist. The great increase in wages which accompanies this type of management will largely eliminate the wage question as a source of dispute.' (91, p. 143) The 'market' aspirations of workers were to be financed out of the higher profits resulting from a complete recapture by management of control over 'managerial' relations. Given existing pre-scientific methods, however, it was understandable and even praiseworthy that workers should try to improve the terms and conditions of their employment. As long as managers so organized production that they were unable to pay high wages, the attraction of unionism would remain.

There is, therefore, a certain tension in Taylor's writing. In his prescription for industrial well-being he upheld the rights of management as absolute in all areas of the employment relationship. In his description of the industrial system of his own time he was prepared to concede that workers might pursue their economic goals through labour organizations. Indeed, the practice of adopting certain elements of the Taylor system while renouncing others — in particular the combination of time study with rate-cutting — was a perpetual source of embarrassment to him; hence he included in his contracts the stipulation that 'the company must do as I tell them', and he reserved the right to withdraw his services 'in case they refuse to follow my instructions'. (6, p. 280n) As Bendix says, 'he certainly tried to make a good case against the abuse of his system by the employers. His natural bias in favour of the employers, however, made him often insensitive to the existence of such abuses.' (6, p. 281n) What is equally important, he was more concerned to condemn managerial delinquency than to account for it. He does not explain why some managements should use his system so selectively that it was certain to misfire. He does speak frequently of the laziness and incompetence of managers as of workers, but how these evils are to be eliminated he does not say. Will managers ever act properly according to the canons of Scientific Management, or must they be spurred continually by a body of Taylorite vigilantes? And who will stimulate the stimulators? All this is, furthermore, less than encouraging from the point of view of the worker, who has been told that unions will be superfluous under Scientific Management. Why should workers trust that managers will not combine time-study with rate-cutting? Would they be well advised to dismantle whatever organizations they have formed to shield themselves from abuses of managerial power? In his own dealings with managers Taylor protected himself; how, then, could he counsel workers to do otherwise?

It is worth adding here that one of the reasons Taylor met with opposition from managers was precisely because he aimed to impose on them a corpus of 'scientific' knowledge which would govern their actions and supplant their judgment and discretion. The phrase 'managers must manage' took on an unpleasing aspect once it was recognized that they would incessantly be told *how* to manage. Although their rights were absolute they were not to be given a free hand, since they retained those rights only on condition that they behaved as managers ought.

The doctrine of managerial rights
The modern doctrine of managerial rights has been expressed many times. The National Metal Trade Association's declaration of principles at the end of the First World War included the following passage: 'Since we, as employers, are responsible for the work turned out by our workmen, we must have full discretion to designate the men we consider competent to perform the work and to determine the conditions under which that work shall be prosecuted, the question of the competency of the men being determined solely by us. While disavowing any intention to interfere with the proper functions of trade unions, we will not admit any interference with the management of our business.' (6, p. 269) A more recent statement of this argument was made in 1956 by the National Association of Manufacturers: 'Putting issues which are strictly the responsibility of management through the compromise procedures of bargaining can only result in undermining management's ability to function effectively.' (1, p. 216)

Although both these examples are drawn from American sources it is hardly surprising that the same opinions are often voiced by British managers. An enlightening illustration is provided by an exchange between the Director-General of the Engineering Employers' Federation and a member of the Donovan Commission. The latter had pointed out that in a sense anything that a trade union does is restrictive, since it circumscribes management's freedom of action. If, for instance, a union succeeds in a claim for higher wages or for shorter hours of work, then the employer is bound to abide by the agreement. This is what was said:

B. Macarty: I do not agree with Mr. Clegg at all that the agreements for minimum rates are restrictive, or that hours of work minima are restrictive, and they are not at all. We have agreements on hours of work providing for overtime, and other things.

H. Clegg: That is restrictive, because if you go beyond them you have to pay a different rate.

B. Macarty: That is not a restriction, that is a concession. (26, p. 747)

In these examples it emerges quite clearly that the improvement of market relations is seen as a legitimate target, while intervention in managerial relations is not. The former is a proper function of trade unions, from which may result concessions by management, the latter is restrictive.

There are two arguments which are usually advanced in favour of the doctrine of managerial rights. First, it is sometimes claimed that once a contract of employment has been signed the employer has the right to dispose of his 'property' as he sees fit: he may do as he likes with his own. More commonly, however, the doctrine is defended by invoking the national interest. Managers are assumed to be engaged in the sedulous pursuit of maximum profit through the most efficient organization of production. Any design by a trade union or unofficial work group to trespass upon managerial functions is likely to jeopardize efficiency. Since they impede the pursuit of maximum efficiency restrictive practices are ever unwelcome to managers and will be accepted, reluctantly, only if the balance of power between labour and capital is unduly weighted in favour of the former. On the question of profit-maximization, and therefore on that of restrictive practices, management forms a united front. Individual managers may well disagree about the details of the means by which maximum profit is to be achieved, but they are at one in opposing obstacles to its attainment. There is no sub-group within management that has an interest in the perpetuation of any restriction; thus the (often unreflecting) hypostatization of 'management' or 'the firm' does no violence to the realities of the industrial situation. From all this it follows that if the national interest is equated with industrial efficiency then restrictive practices are to be condemned; and if it is recognized that certain restrictions may be justified in particular circumstances by an appeal to criteria other than that of efficiency, one can at least hold that restrictions are to be considered *prima facie* against the public interest, as are practices defined by the law to be in restraint of trade. The phrase 'restrictive practices' does not denote a value-free analytical tool: it is a pejorative term resting on the moral foundation of the doctrine of managerial rights. Restrictive practices are arrangements which are fit to be eliminated.

One very striking and basic flaw in this doctrine is shown in Sykes' account of the nature of restrictive practices, where he says that they are actions which 'directly restrict output or which restrict management in their use of conditions or methods which they *believe* would increase the general efficiency of their plant'. (89, p. 239) The trouble here is, of course, that while a firm may have established itself as a monopoly as far as the market for its product is concerned, it cannot monopolize the truth. Managers' beliefs are susceptible to error. What, then, if managers ever deceive themselves about the correct path through the strait gate of maximum efficiency? In such a case a restrictive practice may promote rather than hinder the efficient organization of production. Donald Roy came to this conclusion in his famous series of studies of output restriction in a machine shop. 'Does it not appear', he writes, 'that operatives and their allies resisted managerial "logics of efficiency" because application of those "logics" tended to produce something less than "efficiency"? Did not worker groups connive to circumvent managerial ukase in order to "get the work out"? . . . May not the common query of industrial workers, "What in the hell are they trying to do up there?" be not merely reflective of faulty communication but also based on real managerial inadequacy, quite apart from a failure in "explanation"? May it not be assumed that managerial inefficiency is and has been for some time a serious problem for those who labour?' (83, pp. 377-8) Some practitioners in the Human Relations school argue that communications are important not only because they improve the worker's appreciation of the reasoning behind managerial decisions but also because workers have fruitful ideas that could improve the organization of production. For example, in pressing the virtues of plant-wide incentive schemes W. H. Whyte proclaims that they bring into being 'a more efficient mobilization of the knowledge and ideas of all members of the organization'. (102, p. 105) If for one reason or another managers fail to take advantage of this fund of experience, and if workers carry their own ideas into practice in order to offset the edicts of an incompetent management, who is to say that profit-maximization has been baulked?

A practice may thus be 'restrictive' in that it thwarts the plans of management even though it is not a restriction on efficiency. One reason for this, I have argued, is that managers' plans may be misconceived. Both Taylor and the Webbs were uneasy about managerial behaviour; both cast round for an external stimulus to speed it in the right direction. Moreover, in the wider context of the economy of the nation a restrictive practice may serve a useful purpose. Thus it was seen in the first chapter that apprenticeship ratios may prevent uninformed entry into a declining occupation, producing thereby an improvement in the allocation of the economy's resources. The crucial point is that once it is admitted that such encroachments on 'managerial' functions may be beneficial to the firm or to the country, the usual justification of managerial rights in terms of the national interest is seriously weakened. And if it is stipulated that such encroachments are 'restrictive' simply by virtue of their being encroachments, then it is no longer possible to build into the definition of restrictive practices the assumption that their effects are harmful. Even if we were to follow Hartman's definition by conceding that restrictive work rules are inefficient in the sense that other than least cost combinations of factor inputs are required, it does not follow that the allocation of resources is less efficient than it would have been in the absence of the rule. For the pre-rule allocation may have been non-optimal owing, for instance, to the presence of elements of monopoly or monopsony, elements which the economist would like to assume out of existence. (44, pp. 42-3)

Efficiency is not, however, the only thing of value in the employment relationship. Even the Webbs were prepared, despite their firm preference for the device of the common rule, to countenance restriction of numbers in certain circumstances. This was because they recognized that the untrammelled play of market forces under perfect competition could drive wages down below subsistence level and create unpleasant insanitary conditions and exhausting hours of work. Their conclusion, rebarbative though it was for them, was: 'If, therefore, we had to choose between perfect "freedom of competition" and an effective but moderate use of the device of restriction of numbers . . . the modern economist would hesitate long before counselling a complete abandonment of the old device.' (98, p. 712)

In more recent writings one finds the same reluctance to condemn every practice that obstructs the designs of management. Definitions of restrictive practices include, as a result, an escape clause. The Secretariat of the Donovan Commission exempted arrangements which were 'justifiable on social grounds'; (25, p. 47) the National Joint Advisory Council allowed for the 'reasonable protection of workers'; (30, p. 223n) the Devlin inquiry into the docks declined to proscribe practices 'reasonably designed to secure safety'; (22, p. 11) Weinstein acclaimed ' "reasonable" union rules'; (101, p. 45n) and Northrup championed the importance of 'human aspects and needs'. (78, p. 5)

One knotty problem is to specify the criteria by which 'reasonable' rules are to be distinguished from the 'unreasonable'. Northrup tells us that we must ask: 'Does the benefit to the employees exceed the cost to the employer? The answer can be clear in some cases, subjective or a matter of opinion in others.' (78, p. 5) Now, that one can conceive of an abundance of criteria by which specific rules and practices of labour might be condoned — they may uphold safety precautions, prevent long hours, ensure adequate rest periods, soften the effects of unemployment, guarantee relatively stable earnings from week to week, and so on — and that it is hard to decide how vital each of these justifications is, gives rise to the suspicion that the cases in which the answer to Northrup's question is clear will be swamped by those in which it is subjective or a matter of opinion. As for the cost to the employer, this can no doubt be expressed in principle in financial terms, though in practice it would present serious and perhaps insuperable difficulties. Lupton's investigation of output restriction at 'Jay' Engineering Company was hampered by the impossibility of comparing actual output with maximum possible output, a comparison that has to be made if we are to answer Northrup's master question. For the level of output which managers expected to achieve was not based on the assumption of *perfect* work-flow and *fullest* co-operation from workers. Instead, managers aimed at what Lupton calls a 'social optimum': far from being formed *in vacuo* their expectations had been adjusted in the light of the utilization norms of the work group. The idea of a fair day's work had emerged from tacit negotiations. In any case, the elaborate 'fiddles' practised by the workers meant that the managers of the plant lacked adequate records of the way in which time was spent. They were quite unable reliably to estimate either the amount of time 'wasted' or the direct labour cost of any item. (64, p. 168)

As far as the benefit to the employees is concerned, this cannot be reduced to a simple money equivalent even in principle, let alone in practice. A further problem is to decide whether to assess short- or long-run costs and benefits. If the latter, then how long is the long run? In the light of these difficulties it is regrettable but perhaps not astonishing that those who introduce into their discussion of restrictive practices the concept of reasonable union rules rarely take the trouble to explain in any detail what are the criteria of 'reasonableness' and what is the relative importance of each criterion.

The admission that efficiency of operation is not the sole value involved in the employment relationship leads straight to a further question: *who is to decide* what is reasonable? In the absence of a fraternity of experts equipped with arcane techniques that enable them to discover shared norms of equity we are left with a power struggle. In Fox's words: 'As soon as we recognize that where human and social values are involved there is no one scientifically discoverable "correct" solution, we are knee-deep in claims for democratic representation of those who will be directly affected by whatever solution is chosen.' (32, p. 44) In a democratic society, or in a society in which the ideal of democracy is not treated as an adiaphoron but is regarded as something never attained but always worth striving for, or even in a pluralist society characterized by institutional checks to power, it is incongruous to say that managers should be vested with the right unilaterally to determine what is and what is not reasonable in the relationship between themselves and their subordinates.

The consequences of managerial rights

If these objections are accepted one may be inclined to think that they prove too much. For if the doctrine of managerial rights is no more than a flight from reality, a respectable gloss put upon behaviour, the epiphenomenal smoke (or hot air) over the factory, then although it may be interesting and curious in itself it cannot be used to explain the workings of contemporary industrial relations. This conclusion is, however, unwarranted. From the fact that the doctrine of managerial rights is unclear, inconsistent and often compromised in practice, it does not follow that it can have no effect on behaviour. Most belief-systems are more vague, ambiguous, muddled, muddy and internally inconsistent than is often claimed in the writings of sociologists and social anthropologists. In this respect the doctrine of managerial rights is hardly unique. Its impact on industrial relations is extensive.

In her study of subcontracting in American firms, Margaret Chandler found that the doctrine of managerial rights was frequently abandoned. 'In terms of day-to-day relations among those inside and outside the firm the really basic property concept for management and workers alike involved not absolute notions such as rights, but rather the notion of equity — was one receiving a fair share of current activities, a fair share of the work available? . . . In effect, rights often became a grander cause with which to associate one's concept of a fair share.' (15, p. 309) Managers relinquished in practice their strict devotion to what Chandler calls 'the wins-losses management rights erosion model' — the view, that is to say, that workers' demands were spreading into all manner of areas previously unsullied by their touch, and that this was *ipso facto* an attack on the rights and interests of management. The main result of the doctrine was found to be that it engendered a legalistic approach to labour relations, legalistic in the degenerate sense that form was more important than substance: what mattered above all was that managers should retain at the least the appearance of unilateral control. So it was that during the course of her inquiry Chandler was told by an Industrial Relations Officer that 'anything in writing represents a basic weakness in exercising prerogatives.' (15, p. 104) The Vice-President of one large company was dismissed because he had issued a letter of intent in response to a union complaint, even though the assurances he gave in that letter conformed to the company's policy.

In the engineering industry in this country, the lock-out of 1922 ended in a general reassertion of managerial prerogative, especially the right to decide on the working of overtime. The preamble to the agreement on disputes procedures in engineering opens with a vigorous insistence on managerial rights: 'The Employers have the right to manage their establishments and the Trade Unions have the right to exercise their functions.' (19, p. 236) The agreement itself allows managers to introduce changes in work practices even despite protests from workers, who are obliged to carry their objection through procedure in order to seek redress. The character of procedure in the engineering industry is shaped largely by an attempted adherence to the doctrine of managerial rights. Unlike disputes procedures in most other sectors, where issues are decided by joint bodies whose members are drawn equally from the union and managerial sides, central and local conferences in engineering have had committees made up solely of employers to adjudicate on disputes. It has been pointed out that this procedure, with its authoritarian emphasis on 'employer conciliation', has little effect on the final outcome, for the judgement of any committee requires the assent of the unions concerned; otherwise, the result is a failure to agree. Nevertheless, the arrangement affects the tenor of the proceedings and is not favourable to conciliatory attitudes. Clegg argues that the engineering system has been less successful and less popular than other methods of settling grievances. First, the balance of opinion among full-time union officers is highly unfavourable to the arrangements in engineering. Second, employer conciliation by the EEF fails to resolve a high proportion of the disputes it handles. Finally, it is a relatively protracted affair. The average time taken for an issue unresolved by an engineering works conference to reach central conference is about three months, and some issues take up to a year. (19, pp 238-40) Nor is there any guarantee, from the figures, that it is the major disagreements — those most likely to create unrest and disaffection among the labour force — that enjoy the speediest resolution. Procedure in the engineering industry, with its emphasis on employer conciliation derived from the doctrine of managerial rights is, by comparison to its counterparts in other industries, unpopular with labour's official representatives, unsuccessful, and slow to settle disputes.

In chapter one I cited the finding by Turner and his colleagues that disputes deriving from the problem of job property rights have taken on an increasing importance in motor vehicle manufacture — which is, of course, a sub-division of the engineering industry — since the end of the Second World War. This recent development is largely as a result, Turner maintains, of a radical change in the expectations of manual workers in regard to the employment relationship. In the years between the two wars, unions and the unofficial workplace organizations of labour were struggling to uphold the level of wages in the face of persistent mass unemployment. After the last war, however, and once fears of a recurrence of the depression or of a slump in trade similar to that which had followed the First World War had abated, the aspirations of workers grew rapidly. They came to regard it as reasonable and legitimate that they should have a say in determining the way in which their work was organized because that work was, in a sense, their property.

The concept of job property rights was in sharp conflict with the EEF's stress upon the inviolability of managerial rights. Turner and his co-authors found that many of the disputes arising from the question of property rights had not been directed into the formal conciliation procedure; and this, they claimed, was understandable 'in the light of the Federation's traditional insistence on the sanctity of "managerial functions" and the exemption of matters other than those related to wages and hours from the unions' bargaining scope'. They were quick to add, moreover, that this insistence is maintained despite 'the very real extent to which it is compromised in practice by workplace understandings and agreements'. (96, p. 342) Disputes over job property rights are settled after a fashion: they are treated 'informally'.

Now, it is notorious that engineering in general and motor vehicle manufacture in particular suffer a high incidence of unofficial and unconstitutional strikes. This is not to be explained merely in terms of the characteristic attitudes of the employers. Prominent among other explanatory factors might be the alienating nature of assembly-line work, the shortage of full-time union officials, the impact of piecework on wage-structures, fluctuating earnings, and the proliferation of unions within any one factory, each with different features — craft, multi-craft, semi-skilled, unskilled, general and breakaway — which makes coherent policies on matters other than basic wage rates very difficult to formulate. This last factor has been played up in journalistic accounts of the ills of the British motor industry to the extent that its significance has been grossly exaggerated. In a recent examination of a sample (not, admittedly, a representative sample) of firms in engineering Marsh, Evans, and Garcia found that very few establishments contained a large number of unions. Most had between one and five, the modal number being two. Nor does the available evidence suggest that the picture was markedly different a decade ago, although there have been some amalgamations of unions in the sector. As Marsh *et al.* conclude, 'the numbers of unions with *de facto* negotiating rights have always been exaggerated in the popular mind'. (71, p. 29)

The wholly unintended consequence of the EEF's stand in favour of managerial rights has been the decline in membership participation in constitutional union affairs and an inability to communicate the concerns and aspirations of the rank-and-file to the official leadership. This divergence of the everyday realities of the situation from the formally prescribed procedures has played its part in the growth of the joint shop stewards organization, which is largely independent of the official organs and which devotes itself mainly to demands for fair wages and to claims to property rights. In short, the attitude of the EEF has helped to nurture the conditions favouring the unconstitutionality of industrial relations in engineering, an unconstitutionality which the EEF is quick to deplore. The desire of workers to participate in the formation of utilization norms is not completely ignored; rather, it is appeased in an *ad hoc,* piecemeal, unpublicized and unsung manner with the unofficial or semi-official representatives of labour on the factory floor. This is the characteristic pattern of industrial relations described and attacked by the Donovan Commission. At the national level there are outdated pedestrian procedures that are constantly evaded, and there are substantive agreements on wage rates that bear only a tenuous relation to workers' actual earnings. National agreements are not so much a framework as an empty shell. Donovan aimed to re-integrate the 'two systems' of industrial relations in Great Britain by building upwards from plant level on the basis of, for example, productivity bargains and job evaluation schemes.

Whether or not one accepts the Donovan analysis and remedies, and whether or not one regards the existence of two systems of industrial relations as undesirable, it is surely incontestable that managements and employers' federations do not like this state of affairs. Ironically, their own ideology has been partly responsible for it; and it is no coincidence that the engineering industry, where the ideology has been deeply entrenched, has been widely diagnosed as a main victim of the malaise.

In Huw Beynon's *Working for Ford* the attitudes of one motor vehicle manufacturer are vividly portrayed. (9) Although Henry Ford himself was mistakenly saluted as a great engineer his originality lay in the extent to which he was able to impose and maintain a rigid unshakeable control over the organization of work and the direction of labour. The early history of the company in the United States was marked by emotionally and physically violent opposition to trade unions, an opposition so thorough that it took until 1941 for the United Auto Workers to establish themselves at Ford, and then only after a strike for union recognition. In Great Britain, the workers at Dagenham won the right to join a union in 1944, again as the direct result of a strike. Even so, the company refused outright to bargain on the shop floor and would negotiate only with national union officers.

It is against the historical backdrop of complacent authoritarianism that one must view the decision to set up a new car plant at Halewood. This venture was attractive to the company for several apparently good reasons. The plant would be located in a region of high unemployment, where the labour force would be particularly vulnerable to management pressure and likely to succumb to it. Expansion in this part of the country would enable Ford to develop patterns of relationship with workers independently of the custom and practice that had grown up in the older car plants. Most of the men employed at Halewood were new to the industry, and a good many had never before experienced factory life and discipline; the management team, in contrast, contained men who had witnessed and fought union encroachments on managerial prerogatives at Dagenham and who were keen to prevent their occurrence at Halewood. Given that unemployment in Lancashire was high while average wages were low, there were many who looked to the Ford factory for employment. The management was able to recruit men very selectively — until, that is, unexpectedly high rates of labour turnover, a recurrent problem in the motor industry, forced a relaxation of some of their criteria for selection. They were searching for stable, adaptable men: men tied down by financial and family commitments, men who had not been troublemakers and who did not come from industries where labour organizations had been strong and solidaristic, men who had a calculative and instrumental orientation to work.

Before the new plant was opened Ford signed an agreement with the AEF and the NUGMW granting them sole negotiating rights for the semi-skilled and unskilled workers in the factory; as a result of some pressure the TGWU was admitted as well. The aim was tightly to circumscribe shop steward activity and to channel negotiations through official procedures wherever possible. Beynon's book chronicles the collapse of this project. Infertile though the soil appeared to be, shop floor bargaining and restrictive practices thrust their way to the surface.

Three

The Nature of Restrictive Practices

At the outset of his *Productivity and Trade Unions* Zweig confessed that he had been obliged to abandon his initial sanguine objective of drawing up a tidy categorization of restrictive labour practices according to their various economic and social consequences. For one thing, the effects of what is assumed to be one and the same restrictive practice vary appreciably from one context to another. Many factors may be involved, including the attitudes of workers, the character and strength of the union, the market position of the firm, the response of managers and the overall state of the economy. This imperils any attempt to construct a list of restrictions which are judged to be so harmful as to warrant intervention by the law. In the second place, a restrictive practice is apt to serve a number of ends even in one isolated situation. Seniority rules are clearly aimed at the minimization of favouritism, but they also protect skills, the market for labour, and wages. They ensure a more orderly career structure at the cost of a loss of initiative. Manning standards plainly represent an effort to ward off the threat of unemployment; at the same time they may prevent slave-driving, make possible high quality work and preserve the size and social identity of a work group within a plant. The apprenticeship system not only limits competition for jobs but also socializes the trainee into the customs of the trade. It may also prevent young men and women from entering declining occupations. The closed shop, lines of demarcation, apprenticeship ratios, bans on piecework, direct restriction of output as a group norm: all these are found to perform a wide range of functions. (105, p. 20)

An examination of some well-known and instructive examples of restrictive practices drawn from the academic literature and from Government inquiries will serve as the introduction to a discussion of the nature of restrictive practices generally, a discussion in which conflicting assumptions will be inspected and assessed.

To prevent rate-cutting under systems of payment by results
The founder and champion of the school of scientific management, F. W. Taylor, was well aware that managements cut rates and that workers respond by output restriction or, as he called it, 'systematic soldiering'. Throughout his works he stressed that only defective managerial policies, of which rate-cutting was one, gave rise to systematic soldiering: piecework is self-stultifying if increased production leads only to a cut in the rate. Scientific Management was seen by its creator as a means by which the principal objectives of labour and management — higher wages and lower costs respectively — could be reconciled. It was not devised to secure a higher level of production without any increase in wages.

The authors of the most comprehensive account of the celebrated Hawthorne experiments, F. J. Roethlisberger and W. J. Dickson, were less perceptive. They stated, ingenuously, that the policy of the Western Electric Company was that piece rates were not revised unless there was a change in equipment or manufacturing process; hence, they argued, the real reason for output restriction could not be that it served as a protection against rate-cutting. In a sense the company did indeed live up to its reputation of never cutting a rate. Its policy was that if a process proved to pay 'too much' the part in question was referred to the engineers for redesign, and a new rate was set on the new part. Management thus had its own idea of how much money workers ought to receive per week, and if this amount was exceeded action was taken to restore the *status quo*. The piecework system was a sham.

Studies carried out by Roy in the United States and by Lupton in Great Britain reached similar conclusions. Workers deliberately restricted output in order to guard against rate-cutting and had devised an elaborate network of controls to ensure conformity to the norm of production.

To guard against overworking

The practice of 'welting' has been fou :d in many ports around the world and was deeply entrenched in Liverpool. To deal with this wasteful custom was one of the goals of the Devlin Report on the port transport industry. Welting meant that each gang divided itself into two groups which worked one hour on and one hour off. During his time off on the welt the worker did as he pleased. All the efforts of the employers to solve the problem had the blessing of the Transport and General Workers Union and all, being founded simply on exhortations to enforce discipline, failed. The persistence of welting at Liverpool can be partly explained by the prevalence of piecework. The men relied on a large amount of overtime to eke out their earnings and the port employers encouraged this by offering a considerable premium for it. In these circumstances, Devlin reasoned, 'The welt can be explained, if not excused, by long hours. Many men are regularly working a sixty hour week and it can be said that this would be far too long for the ordinary man if he were not relieved by the welt.' (22, p. 16) It was discovered that from 1960 to 1965 the Liverpool docker had averaged four more hours of overtime a week than his counterpart in London although he put in fewer hours' work during the normal working week. By means of the welt the docker ensured an adequate level of earnings while avoiding extreme physical fatigue.

The evidence is that the reorganization of the port transport industry since Devlin reported has reduced the extent of welting. It continues, but on a less grand, less organized scale. (104, pp. 215-6)

To soften the effects of a casual system

The 'continuity rule' was another practice that was examined by Devlin and his associates. Where the rule operated a docker was entitled and moreover obliged to complete a job once he had been engaged upon it; in the absence of the rule the casual labourer was hired only for the half-day ('the turn').

The continuity rule went some way towards prolonging the job, increasing the time that a docker was actually earning and shortening his time on attendance money. It secured a minimum stability of employment and earnings, and dealt a blow to favouritism in the allocation of desirable jobs.

Although the continuity rule came to be enforced by the dockers on recalcitrant employers, the rule was not of the dockers' making. With the shortage of labour during the war the port employers had been worried that men would try to work only on the plum jobs. The employers themselves insisted that the continuity rule be framed. The 'cunning of history' is such, however, that they soon looked upon the rule as a restrictive practice. Over the years the definition of a 'job' grew so narrow that mobility of labour on the docks was being badly affected.

The Devlin Court argued that under a casual system of employment the continuity rule should be considered protective rather than restrictive, protective in that it was designed to shield men who were not 'blue-eyed' from the constant menace of under-employment and uncertainty about their likely earnings. The Court added that under a system of normal and regular employment the Continuity Rule would 'cease to be protective and become purely restrictive. There would indeed be no room for it in a system in which there was no free call or allocation.' (22, p. 15) Thus it was recognised that the nature and function of ostensibly the same practice vary according to the wider employment situation of which it is a part.

To uphold the unity and cohesion of the shop floor

In several articles A. J. M. Sykes has argued that some of the restrictions imposed in the printing industry have as their goal the maintenance of the unity of the work force *vis-à-vis* the employer. There are rules laying down the sanctions to be used against members who disrupt the unity of the trade union group by working with non-unionists or under conditions not approved by the union. Other rules enforce unity indirectly by ensuring equality among printers. Equality is a means to an end: the preservation of unity. (89, p. 240)

For example, some unions ban piecework, and work groups

often develop complicated devices to mask differences in the output and efficiency of individual printers. Incentive schemes have been introduced more and more since 1945; nevertheless, some chapels ban them outright, others hedge them with all manner of safeguards, and still others will accept only group incentive schemes. This is not to say that printers insist on an absolute equality of pay, since merit money and other bonuses are common throughout the industry. Such extra payments are, however, based on occupational rather than personal differentiations: the criteria are universalistic. Even bonuses for long service or good work are applicable to every man who has the specified qualifications.

Printing is not the only trade where this orientation prevails. Elsewhere, one finds a similar opposition to piecework, to incentive schemes and to bonuses, for the reason that these may divide workers one against the other and weaken their unity in negotiations and disputes with management. A survey conducted by McCarthy and Parker found that a change to time rates was favoured by just over one half of those shop stewards the majority of whose members were paid by results. Prominent among the explanations given for their preference was an awareness that piecework systems create inequalities in pay which may undermine the solidarity of the rank-and-file. (67, p. 43) Zweig found that in the building and civil engineering industry there was deep-rooted opposition to the incentive scheme of October 1947. Trade unionists regarded the bonus system as a threat to their own principles, afraid that incentives would create dissent and jeopardize solidarity; craft unions feared slave-driving and scamped work; many men complained of the arbitrariness of bonuses. Even employers were split on the issue. (105, pp. 78-9)

There is another side to the picture. McCarthy and Parker found that 'about thirty per cent (of unionists) were on some system of payment by results. A third of those employed on such systems said they would like to see them replaced by time rates. About a half of those employed on time rates who thought it would be possible for them to be paid by some other method said they would be in favour of a system of payment by results.' Shop stewards, presumably highly conscious of the need for unity, were keener to replace payment by results than either management or union members. (67, p. 44) The highly efficient worker, at least, may stand to gain financially from a piecework system. To outlaw such methods of payment has, then, disadvantages as well as attractions. Sykes' account of the printing industry is too one-sided; for even in that sector there has long been a conflict between those unionists who favour 'stab (time rates) and those who advocate payment by results.

To heighten the authority of the trade union

In an article on the nature of contemporary collective bargaining Fox and Flanders draw a distinction between the internal and the external strength of trade unions. 'The first is expressed in the strength of a union's internal membership sanctions, its power as an organization over its members, its means of securing compliance with its decisions. The second lies in the external sanctions it can bring to bear on employers to compel them to observe agreements.' (35, p. 155) Their point is that these two aspects of union power tend to vary directly with one another, so that anything which strengthens a union in its dealings with management is likely to enhance its authority over its own rank-and-file members. The closed shop is one device which performs these twin functions.

That a closed shop is operated in a given industry obviously makes any threat of expulsion from the union a potent weapon, more so if it is necessary to have served an apprenticeship in order to secure a job. The craftsman who has spent five or six years on the reduced pay of an apprentice, who now enjoys the privilege, status, relative independence and financial advantages associated with the crafts, and who is aware that there are no non-union shops in the trade (or very few) is not the sort of man flagrantly to break the rules and injunctions of his union. He does not court the danger of expulsion since he has too much to lose.

Admittedly, expulsion from a union is a weapon whose use is infrequent; equally, most union members remain broadly ignorant of the contents of their rule-book. From this it does not follow, however, that the menace of expulsion is illusory and the rules otiose. For as McCarthy points out, disobedience of the union in an open shop might lead to a loss of friendly society benefits and to social ostracism, while disobedience in the closed shop can, if the worst comes to the worst, mean being forced out of the trade altogether. 'It is an awareness of this general contrast, rather than any detailed knowledge of the penalties prescribed for disobedience in the union rule book, that helps to uphold union discipline.' (65, p. 103)

To stamp out favouritism

The continuity rule in the docks, discussed above, was designed not only to guarantee a stable level of employment but also to ensure distributive justice in the allocation of attractive jobs. Where the rule applied a docker was obliged to complete the job he had begun, and this prevented gangs from selecting the good jobs and constantly avoiding the unappealing ones. Each gang was compelled to take the rough with the smooth.

Seniority rules, too, aim at the elimination of favouritism. In the steel industry strict promotion control is enforced by the Iron and Steel Trades' Confederation. Each works, and even most production departments, have quite distinct and specialized work groups, each with its own promotion ladder. New entrants to any plant, usually whether or not they have been employed previously in the industry, will begin at the grade of labourer and will move up the promotion ladder only as they acquire seniority and as posts become vacant. Even though managements tend to reserve the right to veto the automatic promotion of a manifestly incompetent workman it still remains true that the seniority rule dominates the production side of the steel industry.

Hunter, Reid, and Boddy conclude that the seniority principle in the steel industry gravely impedes the mobility of the production labour force. Consequently, important and economically necessary plans for redeployment between and even within plants are often stultified. (50, p. 171) In spite of this, Zweig discovered during his interviews with managers that the straightforward portrait of seniority rules as a harmful restrictive practice often met with little enthusiasm from the management side. ' "Seniority rules are the finest thing in our industry and the mainstay of good labour relations", they would say, "although their application may sometimes be too stringent".' (105, p. 17)

The Webbs were mistaken when, contrasting industry with the civil service and the armed forces, they wrote: 'The very conception of seniority, as constituting a claim to advancement, is foreign to trade unionism.' Although unions might try to protect the vested interests of those already employed in their trades, the Webbs reasoned, there was no idea that promotion should go to the oldest or longest-serving members. (98, pp. 493-4)

Restrictive practices — rational or irrational?
There is, as might have been expected, much argument about the nature of restrictive practices. First, where do they come from? A common answer, and one that is especially popular among economists, is to hold trade unions largely responsible. Thus Weinstein's definition of restrictive practices is formulated in terms of 'union rules'. (101, p. 45) Northrup defines restrictions as 'attempts on the part of unions . . . to interfere with the most economic utilization of labour and equipment'. He goes further: 'The avowed purpose of restrictive labour practice is, of course, to force employers to increase (or not to decrease) the number of jobs controlled by a particular union', (78, pp. 5-6) a purpose that is sometimes hard to square with attempts by craft unions to restrict entry into the trade.

Employers and their organizations are often found to express similar opinions about the origin of restrictive practices. In its written evidence to the Royal Commission on Trade Unions and Employers' Associations, the Engineering Employers' Federation spoke of restrictive practices as 'union insistence on unreasonable manning practices' and 'union limitations on earnings'. The Federation apparently failed to perceive that some of the detailed examples cited in its own evidence had nothing to do with the policy or rules of any union. (19, p. 284) Nor have several of the restrictive practices discussed in the first part of this chapter. 'Welting' in the docks received no support from the Transport and General Workers' Union, which unequivocally blamed the attitudes of the employers for the continuance of the practice. Trade unions played no part in the direct restriction of output revealed in the work of Mayo, Roethlisberger and Dickson,

Roy, and Lupton. The only labour organization at Hawthorne, it should be noted, was a company union. The response to piecework and other incentive schemes in the printing industry differs from one chapel to the next. Systematic overtime is another case in point. The unions are few that omit to denounce the unnecessary working of overtime and to call for a reduction in the working week. Nevertheless, the practice is known to be widespread. It is essentially a *workplace* institution, dependent upon established expectations of earnings which partly derive from the workers' past experience and the level of wages prevailing in the district.

The perspective of Human Relations concentrates to a far greater extent on the 'unofficial' or 'informal' work group as a source of restrictive practices. Since the disciples of this school tend to play down the importance of trade unions this is hardly a matter for surprise. However, the work group is seen less as a bargaining unit — a discrete group of workers with similar skills, traditions, aspirations and interests, and one which tends to remain united on questions concerning the organization of work — than as a friendship clique or tribal society in miniature.

A classic (though admittedly early) study in the Human Relations mould is the celebrated Hawthorne experiment, carried out in a factory in Chicago in the 'twenties and early 'thirties by a team of social scientists from Harvard. Although many subsequent writers have concentrated on serious flaws in the conduct of these investigations, few (John Goldthorpe is a notable exception) (37) have commented upon the debt owed by the Harvard team to the sociology of Vilfredo Pareto, whose work was interpreted for them by L. J. Henderson.

Throughout the body of his celebrated lectures in 'Concrete Sociology' Henderson stressed that the social scientist had the task of penetrating thickets of rationalizations in order to arrive at men's real reasons for action. The stated beliefs and intentions of social actors should normally be taken with a pinch of salt. 'Very often', Henderson's audience was told, 'it is not the meaning of the uttered words that is important, but the attitudes and sentiments that they reveal. I repeat; many things — in many circumstances, most things — that men say are neither true nor false; they are expressions of hopes and fears, of anxieties and obsessions, of likes and dislikes, of aspirations and discouragements.' (46, pp. 81-2) Rarely did social scientists fully realize, in Henderson's view, that the reasons for expressed beliefs were normally hidden and were more significant than the manifest content of the statements.

Henderson's rendering of Pareto was taken on board by the sociologists engaged in research at Hawthorne. This becomes most obvious in their account of output restriction among the men in the bank wiring room. The reasons given by the men for their restrictive practice were that they feared redundancy for themselves and their fellow workers and that they wanted to stop the management from cutting piece rates. Roethlisberger and Dickson were quick to discount these reasons on the ground that: 'Not one of the men had ever experienced any of the things they claimed they were guarding against, yet they acted and talked as though they had.' (82, p. 532) The authors concluded that fear of redundancy and rate-cutting was 'merely the way in which they rationalized their behaviour'. (82, p. 535) In his version of the outcome of the Hawthorne study Henderson repeated their argument with evident approval. That argument is, however, feeble. For one thing, as I have said, management at Hawthorne did cut rates, albeit 'indirectly' and as surreptitiously as they could. But even if the workers had not experienced redundancy and rate-cutting, this still could not show that it was something other than the threat of these possibilities that motivated their output restriction. For if a man gave as his reason for not smoking a wish to minimize the risk of lung cancer and bronchial disorders we could not justifiably laugh his explanation out of court merely because he had always been a non-smoker. Or again, do we have to experience thermo-nuclear war in order to know what it would involve and in order to make talks about strategic arms limitation a rational undertaking? Surely prevention is better than cure in both cases? Only someone over-eager to see reasons as rationalizations could be swayed by Roethlisberger and Dickson's argument.

Henderson had firm views about the problem of introducing changes in the organization of work. He emphasized that managerial plans tend to interfere with 'the little spontaneous social systems . . . that spring up among the workmen. So it often comes about that the workmen are strongly disposed to resist all change. Indeed this is sometimes the chief cause of dissatisfaction among workmen.' (46, p. 135) Whatever reasons workers might give for their opposition to new methods of work, and however plausible their stories might be, those reasons were no more than rationalizations masking an unreasoned, blind adherence to the *status quo* and an irrational fear of change itself. To these largely groundless fears managers were quite insensitive, which was understandable given that managers themselves were a self- and naturally-selected elite who welcomed change and felt no menace from it. Managers, like politicians, 'tend especially to disregard the persistent aggregates of everybody, for they are recruited by a process of natural selection which at present tends to eliminate men possessing certain kinds of strong persistent aggregates and they are often not aware of the strength of these persistent aggregates in the great masses'. (46, p. 136) Broadly speaking, what Pareto meant by persistent aggregates was the tendency many people have to resist social change and innovation and to cling doggedly to the existing social order. So it is that much of the literature of Human Relations interprets workers' resistance to change as unreflective.

We are told by the Hawthorne researchers that workers are guided by 'the logic of sentiments'. In *Management and the Worker* Roethlisberger and Dickson say that they mean by this the 'system of ideas and beliefs which express the values residing in the interhuman relations of the different groups within the plant.' (82, p. 567) They are pointing to the importance of values: to notions of fairness and justice, of correct procedure and due process, of kindness and consideration, of rights and obligations, of privileges and favours, of the dignity of labour, and so on. These are, of course, moral concerns; and it should come as no surprise than men and women see a moral dimension in the employment as in any other social relationship. As the authors say, this is not irrational but social behaviour. Furthermore, in so far as a moral question is salient for an individual it will be likely to generate some emotional charge. People become angry or indignant when they feel that their rights are being denied, or that they are not being treated fairly and with proper consideration. The point about Roethlisberger and Dickson's argument, however, is that they slip easily into the position that each particular pattern of behaviour has its own 'emotional significance' susceptible to an analysis by psychological techniques which will expose the rationalizations and dispel the neurosis. Moral agents thus become suitable cases for treatment.

At one point in their book, when they are considering the outcome of the massive programme of personal interviews carried out at Hawthorne, Roethlisberger and Dickson distinguish three kinds of complaint expressed by workers. (82, pp. 257-263) The examples they give of each type are: *A* 'the doorknob is broken'; 'this machine is out of order'; 'this tool is not sharp'; *B* 'the work is dirty'; 'the lockers are insanitary'; 'the job is dangerous'; 'the work is hard'; 'the room is too hot'; and *C* 'rates are too low'; 'earnings are not commensurate with length of service'; 'ability doesn't count'. In the case of the first type of statement there are commonly accepted criteria for determining whether or not it is false. In marginal cases there might be some scope for disagreement: the doorknob may be hard to budge though the door can still be opened with an effort, the machine may work under protest, and the tool may be used if special attention or force are forthcoming. Nevertheless, there is not much room for fundamental differences of opinion: they are all empirical matters to which readily obtainable factual evidence is directly relevant. As for statements of type 'B', empirical evidence in support of the can be brought forward although we should have to be prepared to tolerate no little disagreement. For example, some people prefer to work in lower temperatures than do others, just as some people prefer to have the windows of their railway compartment closed in order to avoid draughts while others would welcome some fresh air. By the use of an accurate thermometer we can at least determine what the temperature in different parts of a room actually is, and we might expect broad agreement about minimum and maximum acceptable temperatures. Statements of type 'C', finally, are moral judgments that are obviously not verifiable by direct appeal to factual evidence in the same way as one discovers whether doorknobs are broken. Moral disputes have a different character from factual ones. If, for example, Roman Catholics and Protestants disagree about the moral implications of the use of contraceptive devices we should not expect medical evidence necessarily to solve the problem, although it might help to clarify some aspects of it. Likewise, no amount of investigation by social scientists will solve moral arguments about the proper level of piece rates or about the way in which wages are to be linked to merit or to seniority.

The distinctions between the three types of complaint are conceptual, drawn up from first principles. Yet Elton Mayo — and at times Roethlisberger and Dickson — present them as if they were empirical conclusions derived from the Hawthorne experiments. Mayo writes that although criticism of the working environment (i.e. complaints of the first two kinds) proved to be often justified, 'complaints about persons, or for that matter about supervision, in the great majority of instances had to be disregarded . . . the validity of the external reference was minimal'. (72, pp. 92-3) Having, presumably, decided in his own mind what was fair, just and reasonable, Mayo felt able to trace deviance from his own opinion back to the sources of personal frustration that cause workers to misrepresent their relationship to other people. (It is worthy of note that Roethlisberger and Dickson argue against imposing one's own notions of fairness by fiat.) (82, p. 260) Moral disagreements among workers about the conduct of their supervisors and other features of working life are interpreted as good evidence of workers' irrationality. What was originally a conceptual point — that moral arguments cannot necessarily be resolved by an appeal to the facts — becomes an empirical generalization to the effect that workers' moral judgments are usually grossly distorted or simply mistaken. Such judgments are, Roethlisberger and Dickson remark, primarily a product of 'daydreaming, revery, fantasy, and preoccupation'. (82, p. 259) Hence the authors who drew up the conceptual distinctions in the first place are soon worrying about 'concealed, perhaps unconscious, disturbances in the employee's situation'. (82, p. 266) The 'logic of sentiments' turns out to be the irrationality of prejudice and distortion. Moral differences are seen neither as clashes of ideals nor even as the outcome of conflicts of interest.

Despite their frequent use in the literature of sociology the concepts of rationality and irrationality are more than ordinarily unclear. The usual practice is to collapse a number of meanings into one and then to shift from one meaning to another as convenience dictates. Of course, we could make 'rationality' mean whatever we like. It would, perhaps, be odd to stray too far from the everyday meaning of the term or to ignore completely its derivation from the Latin *ratio* (reason). What we should seek is a definition that is precise, internally consistent, and that allows us to generate answers to interesting questions without defining problems out of existence. For the sake of parsimony and in order to avoid misleading other people we should distinguish rationality from other concepts with which it is often confused, e.g. logicality.

My aim here is rather different. This is not a book about rationality, and I shall neither offer a stipulative definition of my own nor choose from among those that are currently up for sale. The aim is to understand what is at stake when people who write about industrial relations use the term in what are often polemical works containing explicit or implicit prescriptions for change.

Two points need to be cleared up at the outset. First, irrationally held beliefs and the actions based upon them are not invariably harmful either to an individual or to his society. Take, for example, the Zande belief system, examined by Evans-Pritchard in a classic of social anthropology. Like more modern belief-systems such as Freudianism, Marxism and astrology, Zande beliefs formed a tightly interconnected, unshakeable whole. The system incorporated logical contradictions that the Azande scarcely recognized and in which they showed no interest. The use of oracles as forms of divination and prediction was protected against any possibility of refutation. If a prediction turned out to be false this was attributed to some irregularity in the ceremony that had been performed: thus the falsification of predictions did not lead to the overthrow of the belief-system itself. Nevertheless, there is no suggestion in Evans-Pritchard's book that Zande beliefs were socially dysfunctional. On the contrary, Evans-Pritchard himself found that they were very easy to live by.

Returning to the Hawthorne experiments and to the sociology of Pareto, Pareto himself did not confuse rationality with social utility. While the underlying objective of his work was to expose the real reasons for human action he did not suppose that his enterprise was necessarily useful. Quite the reverse; had he thought that many people would read his *Treatise* he would not have written it — or so he said. It is only with the later interpreters of Pareto that we see the idea being smuggled in that irrationality is always harmful to its victims. Irrationality was, for them, a barrier to social and economic progress. Pareto did not believe in progress.

Second, rationality is not normally taken to be equivalent to the holding of untrue beliefs. If someone holds a mistaken belief it does not follow that it is an irrational one. When a chess grandmaster conceives a plan that proves to be flawed by a miscalculation we do not rush to decry his move as irrational. When a scientist puts forward an hypothesis that is eventually refuted, again we do not simply say that his belief was irrational. To take another example: cargo cult movements have been found among 'primitive' people who have come into contact with industrial civilizations. The beliefs of the cultists are an effort to explain why the white man possesses so many mysterious and complicated gadgets and yet never appears to make them or indeed to do very much in the way of work at all. The explanation offered for the paradox is, briefly, that the white men receive cargo from the Gods and somehow manage to steal the cargo that was destined for the tribe itself. Now, we are in a position to say with complete certainty that cargo beliefs are false explanations, since we have access to crucial information the cultist lacks. But to say that his beliefs are irrational is quite a different thing.

Rationality refers neither to the truth nor to the social utility of beliefs, but to the process by which individuals arrive at the beliefs which underly their actions. To put the same point another way, the decision whether someone's behaviour is rational or not concerns the way in which one would seek to influence that behaviour and alter it. Thus, if workers' actions are thought to be based on irrationally held beliefs there will be little point in trying to influence these men and women by reasoned argument alone. Managers' reasons will be countered by workers' rationalizations, the result being an impasse, a failure to 'communicate'. On this view one should look to more psychologically manipulative techniques — counselling, interviews, friendly supervision, consultative committees to impart information, piped music and other supposed improvements in the working environment — to influence the norms of the work group so as to bring them into line with those of management. In the Hawthorne study, for example, the contrast between the increasingly productive girls in the Relay Assembly Test Room and the men who restricted output in the Bank Wiring Room lay in the norms each group had developed — the one group placing a premium on hard work and the other not. By creating the right social and physical environment management can influence group norms in desirable directions.

Those, on the other hand, who stress that much of workers' behaviour is rational will not be inclined to rely mainly or even at all upon attempted manipulation. They advocate the use of reasoned argument to persuade workers to behave differently. Just as a chess grandmaster is brought to recognise his mistakes neither by flattery nor by deceit but by the force of valid arguments, and just as natural scientists abandon hypotheses if properly conducted experiments show them to be false, so workers can be swayed by negotiations.

Three approaches to restrictive practices
It is possible and useful to distinguish at least three approaches to the study of restrictive practices. These I shall call the economist's, the human relations and the industrial relations expert's approaches. Although the abstraction involved in producing the three categories inevitably means the simplification of a large body of writings that simplification is not, I believe, excessive. Economics is defined not merely by its supposed subject-matter (either the processes of production, distribution and exchange or, more generally, the problem of the allocation of scarce resources) but also by its characteristic mode of analysis and by the sorts of assumptions and presuppositions on which it rests. There is, among non-Marxist

economists, a certain unity of approach to restrictive practices over-arching the many differences of particular schools of thought. The same is true of academic experts in industrial relations in this country, who have, especially since the Second World War, developed a common orthodoxy about industrial relations problems. As far as the Human Relations school is concerned there is less overall unity. Perhaps what is said here is best applied to Human Relations in the past than to more recent developments.

Restrictive practices are, for economists, normally impositions upon employers by trade unions. They are the product of a reasoned, selfish calculation of sectional advantage. This is not to say that the reasoning is never faulty, and it is certainly not to say that the practices are socially beneficial. They may be neither in the national interest, nor in accord with the will of the majority, nor even in the best long-term interests of the workers themselves. The ultimate goals of restrictive practices are to promote the interests of the union's membership and of the union itself as an organization with interests over and above those of the individuals who make it up. In the former category would be included practices that aim to raise wages, to lighten the work-load, to reduce hours of work and increase the length of holidays, and to ensure stability and security of employment; practices that aim at strengthening the disciplinary power of the union, or that make membership more attractive by penalizing non-members, would fall into the latter category. The two are seen to be intimately related and mutually supportive. For success in winning benefits for workers will make union membership more alluring, and, conversely, a strong union will be more effective in winning benefits.

The comparison is drawn with restrictive trade practices, which are agreements between firms in the same market whose object is to decrease competition, thereby providing the firms with greater security, an easier life and excess profits. Restrictive trade practices may take the form of direct price-fixing agreements, of agreements about profit margins, of agreements about standards of servicing and guarantees, of agreements to share the market, of devices to stop new competitors from entering the market, and so on. *Prima facie,* restrictive trade practices are against the public interest, since consumers are denied the benefits of wide choice in a truly competitive market. Competition stimulates technological improvements and cost-consciousness; it rewards the efficient and the progressive and punishes the incompetent.

Most economists would concede that restrictive trade practices may be justified in some circumstances. For example, firms may claim that by limiting competition they are able to guard against sudden, unforeseen fluctuations in demand so that they can plan rationally and effectively for the future, and that this in turn enables them to finance long-term fundamental research and to meet demands that otherwise could only be satisfied by importing goods at great cost to the country's balance of trade. They may claim, again, that only by enforcing limits to competition can they maintain the quality of their product. In essence, they make out a *special* case for themselves on economic or social grounds and they remain guilty until proved innocent. Their case should be argued before a tribunal of independent, suitably qualified and well-informed judges who will decide whether the practice is in the public or national interest. If it is not, then it will be prohibited by law. Precisely the same procedure, it is thought, should be adopted to deal with restrictive labour practices. The unfair, socially undesirable practices both of trading and of labour monopolies should be stamped out by legal penalties.

The manager faced with restrictive labour practices is in much the same position, ironically, as the consumer who has to deal with restrictive trade practices. Both are victims of monopoly power. The manager assiduously seeking to maximize profits is baulked by unions, and the consumer — economic man — rationally maximizing utility is hedged about by cartels. They need help against the power that encircles them.

Although there is some support among economists for productivity bargaining many of them have strong reservations. They point to the danger that workers will deliberately hoard new restrictive practices in order to sell them in future rounds of bargaining: thus managers would have to yield more and more concessions simply to maintain efficiency at existing levels with little hope of actually increasing it. Another problem is that of inflation. Through productivity bargains groups of workers achieve wage increases; other groups press for increases in order to catch up or restore differentials, but these groups may not be able, for good or bad reasons, to raise productivity themselves. The process continues, and an inflationary spiral is set in motion as firms pass on increased costs to the consumer. An equally disturbing feature of productivity deals is that they may interfere with the operation of price mechanisms and lead to a misallocation of resources. Increases in productivity, it is argued, are usually the result of using more efficient, capital-intensive (i.e. labour-saving) modes of production rather than the outcome of harder effort by the workers. Hence, in those industries in which productivity has increased there will be a need to cut back on the labour force, or at least to lower the rate of recruitment to the industry. In this situation it would be economic nonsense to pay added incentives to a factor of production, labour, that was less in demand then before.

In the Human Relations tradition, in contrast, restrictive practices are seen as a symptom of strain and not as a manifestation of interests. Men and women suffer strains outside the factory — tensions in personal relationships and, as Mayo for one stressed, a sense of isolation, purposelessness and anomie in an impersonal, urban, bureaucratized society — which carry over to life inside the factory, where frustrations show themselves in irrational responses to the work situation. For Mayo what was needed was the *Betriebsgemeinschaft* — the factory community into which the worker would be integrated, providing him with standards of conduct and a sense of belonging and purpose.

Mayo and his colleagues were eager to overthrow the 'rabble hypothesis' and the notion of 'economic man' as a being who rationally and selfishly pursues his own individual interests. Instead of this picture they presented a view of man as a social animal who seeks gratification from work itself and from personal contacts with fellow workers and with bosses. Workers inevitably form ties of sociability with one another, and, again inevitably, develop social groups with codes of conduct and values of their own. These codes and values are not essentially designed to protect group interests from the depredations of other groups; they are neither more nor less than the social cement that binds society together. The precise make-up of that cement — the content of the group's codes and values — is subject to wide variation. More, it is malleable. Some groups restrict output while others struggle for high and rising levels of productivity. The Human Relations expert has the task of identifying the conditions that produce workers who value high production. The assumption is made that it is possible to create conditions inside the factory that will offset the influence of the worker's position outside it. What style of leadership, 'authoritarian' or 'democratic', should supervisors display? Should channels of communication between managers and workers be improved? Should the working environment be changed to heighten social interaction between workers? What is the ideal size and composition of work groups? Does it help if workers are allowed to choose the people they work alongside? What is the effect of job enlargement and job rotation?

In Human Relations literature, as its critics have often noted, there is a certain insensitivity to the importance of social relationships outside the factory: analysis stops at the factory gates, to be replaced at best by random anecdotes. Socialization in the family and at school, the effect of peer groups, social class, political and religious affiliations, position in the life cycle are treated unsystematically, if at all. These factors, among others, help to shape what Goldthorpe and Lockwood have called the worker's 'prior orientation to work', i.e. the expectations and aspirations that individuals bring with them into the factory. One fruitful research strategy is to attempt to explain variations in behaviour at the place of work in terms of differences in social position in the wider society. (8) Instead, Human Relations plays down the role of cultural and social diversity within and between societies, and tries to adumbrate universal rules that will apply throughout time to all groups of people. In this it is not very different from Taylorism.

The perspective of most students of industrial relations is different again. Although, for them, some so-called restrictive practices are embodied in union rules the majority derive from the workplace situation. Here the work-group is crucial. The work-group is a body with shared interests, traditions and skills, a body that forms a bargaining unit with management. The emphasis on shared interests is one of the key points that sets this view of restrictive practices apart from the Human Relations interpretation. The members may well be friendly and sociable with one another, but this is not, as it is for Human Relations, what binds them together. Restrictive practices derive mainly from the rational pursuit of group interests, and it is for the protection of these interests that group solidarity and group norms develop. To use Goldthorpe and Lockwood's terms, most working-class collectivism is (and always has been) 'instrumental', (41, pp. 38-9) a means to an end.

Squandering resources within the industrial enterprise springs from a number of different situations. It may be buttressed by union rules or by the custom and practice defended by particular work-groups. It may be the result of managerial rules and decisions or of the actions of interest groups within the management structure. Or it may be that the inefficiency of certain working arrangements simply is not noticed by anyone. These last two categories, the argument runs, are very important and greatly neglected. For a basic weakness of the Human Relations and the economist's approaches is that by assimilating restrictive practices to actions by workers and their associations many other sources of waste are left entirely out of the picture. Above all, the narrowing of focus means that the involvement of management is skated over. Managers are seen as profit-maximizers, competent to define restrictive practices and eager to uproot them. 'Restrictive practices', a term used by managers to evaluate unfavourably the behaviour of unions and workers, is incorporated uncritically into the conceptual armoury of various social sciences.

Productivity bargaining tends to be seen as the most fruitful way of dealing with restrictive practices and also of improving efficiency and the quality of industrial life. Ideally it implies discussions not only with trade union officials but also with the work groups and their immediate representatives, the shop stewards. An effort is made to reach a state of common advantage. Workers may receive higher wages, shorter hours, longer holidays, more favourable fringe benefits and so on, while the company will achieve a higher profitability by being able to cut its labour force, by reducing unnecessary working of overtime, by reducing the number of men required to operate particular machines, and by introducing more flexible arrangements for co-operation between different work-groups and unions. Possibly — although this point is less to the fore — consumers may gain through lower prices for the firm's product.

Productivity bargaining is thought to have a liberating and democratizing effect. Groups of managers and workers seek to discover more and more ways of furthering their common advantage: their consciousness is raised and their resources of insight and knowledge are pooled. The productivity deal is not a one-off exercise and the desired common advantage is not merely a short-term once-for-all rise in wages and profits. It is this, argue industrial relations experts, that makes groundless the fear that workers will hoard new restrictive practices. For the *attitudes* of managers and workers will change radically; indeed, attitude change is a precondition of successful productivity bargaining.

If productivity bargaining is to have its desired liberating and democratizing effects then not only attitudes but also organizational structures will have to change. A firm genuinely committed to productivity bargaining *as a new style of management* can no longer treat labour relations as the province of a separate personnel department with the limited and dispiriting brief of clearing up troubles produced by managerial decisions taken without due consideration and proper discussion. Unions, on the other hand, will have to respond by increased co-ordination between themselves and by better internal communications so that supposedly 'joint' decisions are more than a matter of union officials and managers reaching agreement without the consent of the work force. It is this consent that gives agreements both their stability and their legitimacy.

Perhaps management will act only when it is itself spurred on by an external goad. In the case of Fawley, for example, the efficiency consultants played an important part in analysing the nature of inefficiency at the refinery and in convincing the management that steps could be taken to deal with the problems. Again, the parent company was facing severe international competition, and this encouraged it to compare the level of efficiency in its various plants: Fawley showed up badly. Government policies can obviously have an impact on the efficiency-consciousness of the firm, e.g. by insisting that wage rises be covered by increases in productivity as a barrier to inflation. It may well be, then, that it is only within a favourable social and economic context that managers will come to embrace productivity bargaining. On the whole industrial relations experts have not gone far in examining the factors that make up a favourable climate for productivity bargaining. Be that as it may, they have stressed that the initiative for change will normally come from managements and not from unions, since unions are primarily defensive bodies whose aim is first and foremost to defend existing rights and existing privileges. Justifiably and rationally suspicious of change, unions are unlikely to launch themselves whole-heartedly into a campaign to persuade their employers that far-reaching changes can be mutually profitable.

Orthodox schemes for promoting industrial democracy by incorporating workers' representatives into managerial decision-making are viewed with suspicion. Nothing, it is claimed, will be altered in the long run by having these men taking on the functions of managers because they will swiftly become indistinguishable from managers *tout court*. As more and more of their time is consumed by managerial decision-making they will be cut off from the day-to-day contact with their members that is vital to the democratization of industrial relations. At a social-psychological level they will suffer role conflict, which ultimately can be dispelled only be resigning or by abandoning their identification with the men and going over to the management side. Workers themselves, disenchanted by the attitudes and performance of their representatives, will turn to shop stewards and to the well-tried methods of collective bargaining to pursue sectional and individual interests, bypassing the new mechanisms.

A resort to the law to deal with so-called restrictive labour practices is not the road to industrial well-being, in the opinion of the overwhelming majority of industrial relations experts. No just law could ever be framed in sufficient detail to guarantee that only unwarranted restrictive practices would be prohibited. The effects of restrictive practices vary through time and between firms and industries to such an extent that courts would be unable to try every case on its own particular merits. The success of legal prohibitions would depend, furthermore, upon the willing and active co-operation of industrial managements up and down the country. It is they who must bring cases to the courts' attention, and upon their testimony much of the case for the prosecution will rest. The snag is that laws have to be backed by penalties for transgressors if they are to be of any use and if the law itself is not to be discredited. Managers will be understandably reluctant to sour the climate of industrial relations by bringing court proceedings against workers and unions except in the most extreme circumstances. It will be unpleasant, and it will not pay. What many firms would like would be an arrangement by which restrictive practices could be outlawed without the firm's having anything to do with the court action or with the penalties imposed. They might then dissociate themselves from any hostility through the claim that the law stands above manager and worker alike, constraining them both. However, in the absence of an efficient industrial Gestapo there is no way that courts could operate without extensive help from managers.

The literature of industrial relations is more subtle and more acute than its rivals in its analysis of restrictive practices and in its prognoses for industrial health. Instead of rushing to dismiss restrictive practices as irrational it tries first to explain workers' reasons for their actions in terms of the protection of vested interests. It does not have blind faith in the law as a panacea for industrial relations problems. It tries to understand the role played by managers in defining and dealing with restrictive practices. It does not ignore the moral and political aspects of the employment relationship. Restrictive practices are not simply attempts to get more money for less work, nor are they essentially irrational responses springing from frustration, fantasy and revery. They are efforts by workers to exercise some *control* over features of the employment relationship, efforts that can often be analysed in terms of the pursuit of individual and collective interests. A measure of control is both a means to other ends and an end in itself. So in speaking of restrictive labour practices and of the aims of workers and unions we cannot legitimately avoid discussion of the questions of participation in decision-making and of democracy itself.

In this literature there is, however, a general failure to see the conduct of industrial relations in the context of a wider social setting. Writings on productivity bargains, for instance, have tended to play down their influence on other firms and other groups of workers and to turn a blind eye to their inflationary and disruptive consequences. Similarly, the meaning and problems of industrial democracy are discussed with barely more than a passing reference to democracy in other spheres of social life such as the polity and the family. Far-reaching problems have been left to the scrutiny of sociologists, economists and political scientists.

Four

Managers and Professionals

Managers' involvement in restrictive practices
The Webbs, like many of their successors, largely ignored the role of the employer in collective bargaining. Underlying their discussion was the straightforward assumption that the employer is opposed to trade union activities and will resist them to the best of his ability. If this is so, then *a fortiori* he will struggle to prevent restrictive practices, encroachments upon managerial prerogatives. But there are, in fact, many situations where the manager considers that he has a positive interest in the continuance of an unashamedly 'restrictive' practice, given the power politics inherent in industrial management and the ideologies that are partly created by it; what is more, there may be sub-groups in the management team who have attitudes towards restrictive practices different from those of other factions.

McCarthy gives a report of a confidential study that showed that there is often a discrepancy between the officially declared policy of a firm and its actual behaviour when it is faced by demands for the closed shop. At the highest level managers tended to insist that they had never conceded the closed shop, but lower down in the hierarchy it was explained that workers were screened to determine whether or not they were willing to pay union dues. Conscientious objectors were not offered employment. (65, p. 89) Because the closed shop is or is thought to be disliked by the public, employers are frequently prepared to accept it only if they can do so tacitly. It is mainly for this reason that recognition often takes the form of an unofficial understanding rather than being formally incorporated into the contract with the union.

This is not a situation unique to Great Britain. In the United States of America, where the pre-entry closed shop is prohibited by federal law, several of the states have enacted 'right-to-work' laws proscribing the union shop as well. One firm changed its recruitment policy as the result of such a law. (88, pp. 57-8) Applicants were informed not only that the firm and the union concerned had agreed to operate the union shop but also that the state had passed a law forbidding this kind of agreement. It was to be left to the discretion of the applicant whether he should join the union. Clearly, this was a violation of the state law. Even so it did not satisfy the union. The management had to go still further in its flouting of the law. The industrial relations staff simply told each applicant of the agreement with the union and tried to induce him to abide by it. Only if pressed by the prospective employee would the industrial relations officer openly admit that, in law, union membership could not be made compulsory.

Examples such as these do not necessarily betray a capitulation to union demands based on the consideration that, unfortunately, no other course of action is available. Many managers, to the contrary, have been found to admit that the closed shop has advantages from their point of view. Zweig was told that 'employing non-unionists with union members causes a great deal of friction which is unnecessary', and that 'peace in industry is worth paying for'. (105, p. 16) An employer explained to McCarthy that his firm 'found that it helped to have every man in his respective union; in this way local leaders come to feel more secure, and they were more willing to help in putting over management's view to members'. A representative of another company argued that 'it is essential to insist that (the men) must all be in the union, otherwise the stewards will not handle the complaints of the non-unionists'. (65, pp. 92-3) And in a recent survey of a sample of establishments in the engineering industry Marsh and his colleagues found that 'only' 44 per cent of their respondents saw advantages in union shops. (71, pp. 159-160) To many people this figure would be surprisingly high.

A slight difference can be detected here between managerial attitudes to shop stewards on the one hand and full-time union officials on the other. The closed shop means that grievances from the shop floor will be pressed by the stewards in an orderly fashion through the formal channels; meanwhile, the union official will perform a mediatory role as a 'manager of discontent', as one who 'puts over' management's view and prevents the demands of his members from outstripping the capacity to meet them. In spite of this difference, employers and managers who testify to the advantages of the closed shop share one fundamental belief: that the closed shop produces a better disciplined and more tractable labour force. This is a logical consequence of the argument that the external power of a trade union varies directly with its internal strength. Managers will not be likely to relish a growth in the former; nevertheless, they may welcome it if it is counterbalanced by a greater influence of the union over its members. They are faced with a problem. 'If they want the unions to be strong enough to maintain the peace by controlling members' behaviour, they should not complain of excessive union power or propose measures that will have the effect of weakening them.' (35, pp. 154-5) Many will see, then, that they have a positive interest in the maintenance of the closed shop even if they are in no position to confess this in public. To them the non-unionist will be decidedly unwelcome since he represents a potential source of bitter yet avoidable conflict. Such a manger will question an aspiring employee about his attitude to unionism not out of a desire to conciliate the union at all costs, to pay Danegeld, but because he too has a stake in the closed shop.

The way in which overtime operates shows similar processes at work. At the Fawley oil refinery, for example, systematic overtime was used as a means of attracting and retaining labour by ensuring that the wage packet was adequate. There are, of course, other ways of offering inducements, but they may have drawbacks. It may not be possible to supplement earnings by payment by results or bonuses. The alternative of raising basic wages may be incongenial on three main counts: it may conflict with national agreements; it may incur the displeasure of the employers' association, which resents overt competition for labour; and it is thought of as an irreversible step. Policy overtime, on the other hand, preserves the appearance of flexibility, since managers like to believe that they have complete discretion on the working of overtime. Often, however, the flexibility may show itself to be illusory. Once a particular level of overtime per week becomes normal it also becomes the norm. Both managers and workers grow accustomed to it and regard as legitimate any claim that it ought always to be available if anyone wants it. Inertia in the system builds up rapidly.

One might expect that output restriction by workers who are paid by results would place them in unqualified opposition to rate-fixers, first-line supervisors and higher management. Here, if anywhere, we should see open and undisguised conflict over a brazen restrictive practice. That such a conclusion may be unwarranted is shown by Lupton's findings in his research at 'Jay' Engineering Company. Ostensibly, rate-fixers were seeking to make piece rates as tight as they could and were well aware that workers concealed loose rates by the practice of 'cross-booking'. True to type, rate-fixers advocated the policy of introducing a trifling redesign of equipment in order to provide an opportunity to set new and tighter rates. But there were social pressures acting on the rate-fixer that made him deviate from his officially ordained role. Were he to be over-zealous in setting rates workers would complain to their steward, and he in turn would raise the question with management. This could cause great inconvenience to the manager, and he would make his irritation felt to his subordinates, not least to the rate-fixer responsible. The latter soon discovered, therefore, that if he wanted a reasonably untroubled existence he had to abandon the quest for an 'ideal' incentive scheme. Pressure from the workers, writes Lupton, 'transformed him from a pure representative of management into a kind of arbitrator. He was induced to work in terms of what was acceptable, given existing relationships.' (64, p. 151) Thus men whose position symbolizes perhaps more than any other the rational pursuit of business interests — men who were the cornerstone of Taylorite Scientific Management — failed to act as the profit-maximizers of economic theory.

Similar pressures were exerted on foremen, to the extent that sometimes they even advised workers to cross-book. The foreman was expected to keep a record of the exact time workers had taken on each job, but he was far too occupied with his other responsibilities to do any more than investigate flagrant falsifications of daywork and timework sheets. It was not simply a matter of his being too busy: he also had to take account of his relationship to those under him and their expectations about his performance of his duties. Briefly, they expected him not to take too close an interest in their work when all was going smoothly but to be ready to help when problems arose. 'If he behaved otherwise', Lupton tells us, 'he forfeited his moral right to ask for help'. (64, p. 154) Withdrawal of co-operation was a sufficiently dangerous threat to ensure that for the most part the foreman honoured the agreement by not checking too scrupulously the times taken on each individual item.

As Lupton's inquiry proceeded he was driven to conclude that the so-called 'fiddle' could operate successfully only if foremen and time-clerks collaborated. (64, p. 153) So too an investigation conducted in the United States by Roy revealed that even first-line supervisors, who usually adopted the position of silent accessories after the fact, tried to encourage workers to circumvent formal rules and regulations so as to comply with the demands of the 'informal' system, i.e. with the utilization norms of their fellows. One of the foremen went so far as to tell the investigator: 'You've got to chisel a little around here to make money'. (83, p. 369)

In another American study, J. W. Kuhn argued that since first-line supervisors want to avoid loss of production time while maintaining as much independence as possible they are obliged to overcome obstacles raised by the collective agreement, shop rules and customary practices. The better to fulfil their production goals they require a measure of freedom to work out for themselves immediate arrangements in their own departments; in other words, they try to escape intervention by higher management and the industrial relations department, and this in turn implies 'fractional bargaining' with workers and their stewards so as to prevent grievances from coming to the attention of those further up on the managerial ladder. Workers have the ability to cause great discomfort to first-line supervisors and can clog the grievance procedure by the sheer volume of the complaints they submit. The less that higher management, the industrial relations department and the restrictions of the collective agreement are involved in his shop affairs the freer the foreman is; the fewer the grievances that go to the top the less notice is paid of the details of arrangements on the shop floor. (56)

That the pressures acting on foreman may derive directly from management is shown by Slichter and his colleagues. Foremen will try to shirk responsibility and conceal mistakes if management uncritically holds them accountable for the fulfilment of production targets. In one factory where this attitude prevailed the foremen did their utmost to make a good showing on paper. 'They protected their loose standards from discovery; they fought to get looser standards; they devised but did not report shortcuts in production; and they cheated in reporting production.' The ironic outcome of this was that 'those who did well on paper were regarded as the best foremen'. (88, p. 905)

Managerial interest groups

In the studies by Roy, Lupton, and Kuhn there is a suggestion that the aims and interests of various levels of management concerning restrictive practices may not coincide. Unfortunately, it remains little more than a suggestion. Both Roy and Lupton concentrated their attention largely on the patterns of interaction between first-line supervisors and work groups, and had relatively little to say about the attitudes of middle and higher management towards such practices. From Roy's study it is not even clear how far higher managers were aware of the effectiveness of the 'fix' let alone whether or not they were ever prepared to condone it. Lupton does report that the assistant departmental manager at 'Jay' was embarrassed and his authority undermined whenever those responsible for the planning of production failed in their job and thereby invited the charge that management was not really concerned about efficiency. (64, p. 158) Nevertheless, the material in Lupton's study is too scant to provide a detailed assessment of the attitudes of middle and higher managerial levels. Its interest — like that of the investigations by Roy and by Kuhn — lies, rather, in the demonstration that the foreman and to a lesser degree the rate-fixer, both of whom are supposed to be representatives of management, can have a stake in the most incontrovertibly 'restrictive' practices.

The failure to set out differences in attitudes among managerial groups, particularly among men higher up in the scale, derives mainly from the choice of participant observation on the shop floor as a research technique. The method does, admittedly, have some striking advantages. By comparison with many other techniques it is a relatively non-reactive research instrument, i.e. its use does not greatly interfere with the object of the inquiry. The researcher tries to put himself in a position where the very act of his observing other people's actions will not affect their actions in any way. Second, use of this method helps to prevent the researcher from swallowing whole the 'official' version of events, from falling into the trap of deferring to what Becker has called 'the hierarchy of credibility'. (4, pp. 126 ff) In most organizations, as Becker notes, the men and women holding positions of authority are well-placed to convince outsiders that their own view of what the organization is for and what takes place within it and in its dealings with other groups is the correct view. A task for the sociologist is to redress the balance, to call into question bureaucratic categories and official statistics and to paint a picture of the organization as subordinates see it. In this endeavour the researcher may be cut off from all but the lowest levels of management.

The concept of the work group has assumed a central place in the analytical framework of industrial relations and industrial sociology. Few serious investigators would attempt to analyse industrial relations without determining the work groups present in a particular situation and examining their beliefs, perceived interests and behaviour. In spite of this it is still common to treat management as if it were a homogeneous body, the 'management team'. Not every writer does this, of course; and those who do may defend themselves by pointing out that theoretical abstractions help us to see order in the apparent chaos of social life. The question that is crucial for this book is: are there subdivisions within the managerial camp that are relevant to a discussion of restrictive labour practices?

Management Rights and Union Interests by Margaret Chandler helps to provide the answer. In that book, Chandler discusses problems arising from the decision to subcontract maintenance and construction work within a plant to independent contractors. Since the Second World War this practice has become increasingly common in American industry and has often sparked off industrial disputes. To the hard-headed economist or the champion of managerial rights the question whether to employ the services of external contractors is purely one of economic and technical efficiency and is decided on these criteria by management alone. For managers are dedicated to the goal of maximum profit. Any essay by a trade union or work group to make its voice heard on a decision such as this, where norms governing the utilization of resources are at stake, is to be denounced as a restriction on managerial prerogative.

Most people writing about the subcontracting problem portray labour and management as two monolithic units locked in battle. It is clear that this is the view of Slichter, Healy, and Livernash, for they write: 'On the one hand, management regards its rights as very broad, holding that it has the right to subcontract at any time, even operations that have traditionally been integrated. On the other hand, the union maintains that the jobs and work for which it bargained when it was recognized as the bargaining agent and entered into an agreement belong to the union. Because of these sharply disparate views, the problem has proved to be a serious one'. (88, p. 282) Walton and McKersie's discussion is cast in similar terms even though they do realize that motives on both sides may be complex. (97, pp. 133-4) Another authority, W. Gomberg, includes in his analysis the union organizing the external contractor's employees; but the overall assessment remains the same. Only three parties are engaged in the battle: the two unions are in dispute over whose job properties are the victims of trespass, while the employer follows the course dictated by organizational efficiency no matter whose job rights are being infringed. (43, p. 113)

Chandler's analysis was more subtle. She found that: 'There were no united fronts in the contracting-out issue, but rather conflicting interests — diverse systems of rights and equities within each major group.' (15, p. 63) Instead of treating management and labour as the leading protagonists she dissected into component parts the 'inside' group that favoured integration and the 'outside' group that advocated subcontracting. The hard core of the inside interests was found to be the maintenance and construction workers of the plant, their union, *and the departmental manager in charge of them.* Craft workers in the community, their unions and their contractor-employers constituted, in contrast, the hard core of the outside interests. In addition to these there were peripheral groups that were likely to involve themselves in the question. Included among them were associations representing speciality, general and integrated contractors; national craft unions; community officials; general industrial management, and various departments in the firm such as engineering, purchasing, and industrial relations. For example, a plan to introduce an outside maintenance contractor with a nation-wide operation into a modernized process plant may be resisted by a coalition of the industrial plant union and the head of the maintenance department, as well as community officials and general and speciality contractors who wish to see the work assigned to a local contracting company. Pressures in favour of the move may be exerted by top management in the company, the plant engineer, and a contractors' association representing the national group. Such coalitions of interested parties or 'stakeholders' cut across what are normally regarded as the 'organizational boundaries'.

It seems that more and more firms in the United States are changing to a policy of subcontracting maintenance and construction work. This has been due not only to the economic and organizational advantages of the move but also to the fact that the 'outside' interests have tended to possess the more influential supporters. Although Chandler found that the inside group was frequently sustained by some elements at the middle and lower levels of management, top management and others at the middle level have preferred the policy of subcontracting as an appropriate reaction to economic pressures. The insiders, and above all the union organizing the maintenance workers in the plant, have been compelled to look outside for help, e.g. to arbitrators.

The significance of Chandler's work is that it explodes the easy assumption of management as a unified team. Her argument is more than the simple observation that managers tend to disagree about the most suitable means of achieving their common goal of maximum efficiency, or that personal animosities among managers can reduce their collective 'goal-effectiveness'; for these points are disputed by no one. What she does show is that the structure of the industrial organization and the nature of the environment in which it operates and upon which it is dependent may well create a situation where a managerial sub-group has a stake in a restrictive practice. Management, like the labour force, is divided into a number of occupational groupings. Hence, *the concept of job property rights and the doctrine of vested interests apply to managers as well as to workers.* The head of department in charge of the maintenance and construction workers is apt to be as strongly opposed to subcontracting as is the union organizing the men working under him. He can, after all, scarcely be expected to applaud a policy — however nicely it meets the requirements of efficiency — if it threatens to undermine his importance, reduce the rewards he enjoys and possibly make his function redundant. Given that management is a system of interest groups it follows that the outcome of any policy issue will be contingent not solely on the economic merits of the cases for and against it but also on the balance of power between the rival managerial factions. Acknowledgement of this point deals a mortal blow to the doctrine of managerial rights, which draws part of its plausibility and attraction from the assumption that management is a team united in a search for maximum profit.

Evading responsibility for labour relations
Employers, as mentioned earlier, may be glad of a restrictive practice on the ground that it produces a better disciplined labour force. It needs to be noted that this attitude may signify a desire entirely to abdicate any responsibility for labour relations. Thus managers may look upon union officers as men

who will co-operate in 'putting over' management's view to the rank-and-file. A suggestion of a similar approach may be betrayed by the remark of one employer that the concession of the closed shop can 'save a lot of time in dealing with odd, fiddling issues'. (65, p. 93) For if the issues are not really trivial at all in the eyes of the work force then the statement may reveal the lack of an adequate personnel policy. Certainly there is a strong case for saying that British management prefers on the whole to have as little as possible to do with industrial relations. The Donovan Report exposed and condemned the neglect of personnel policy: 'Many firms have no such policy and perhaps no conception of it. (24, p. 25) Other inquiries have underscored the same point. The Cameron Court found that there was 'a dearth of managers with special responsibility for personnel matters' in the printing industry. Little more than a dozen of the establishments affiliated to the British Federation of Master Printers had separate personnel departments — a poor showing, even allowing for the high proportion of small firms in that sector. (13, pp. 70-1) The efficiency consultants engaged by the Shawcross Commission on the Press found that there were 'indications that management appears to be so engrossed with general policy that it devotes insufficient time to current problems of labour utilization'; for instance, it was too often the case that all senior managerial staff had left the office before mechanical production began. (85, p. 216) Marsh's study of the engineering industry showed that despite a growth in professional assistance the staffing of industrial relations at the level of the firm was marked by 'continuing amateurism'; indeed, 'a considerable number of large establishments have no one in charge of personnel acting in a full-time capacity, and the predominance of line management is generally notable'. (71, p. 28) Lord Devlin's inquiry into the port transport industry indicated comparable negligence by employers. Although they denounced restrictive practices the port employers had failed to study their economic and social effects in any systematic fashion and did not even draw a clear distinction between deliberately wasteful practices and those which were no more than bad habits curable by firmer discipline. Having signed an agreement they expected union officials to take sole charge of its enforcement. Devlin rightly stressed the futility of this expectation. 'A union does not, when it makes an agreement of this sort, warrant that all its members will always observe it. What it does is to say that it will not protect them if they do not observe it. A trade union officer is not a policeman who can be called in by the employers to enforce the law'. (22, pp. 20-1)

Chandler found that sub-contracting was double-edged: on the one hand it was a means by which some managements shuffled off their responsibilities, but at the same time it could be used to reassert managerial control and prerogatives by proxy. Subcontracting offered an escape from some of the rebarbative and time-consuming obligations of the employment relationship itself. The external contractor recruited, selected, trained, supervised, disciplined and remunerated his own work force. The management of the plant retained its control over all the essential elements of planning while the peripheral area, which included several potential threats to managerial rights, was allocated to others. In the opinion of a superintendent of industrial engineering: 'Those contractors pay their boys high wages, and they tell them to jump to it or else get out. We would never treat our employees in this fashion. We have to keep up good relations'. In other words, the external contractor would pass on his insecurity to his employees. If the latter proved fractious and if the contractor did not take a firm stand on the sanctity of his own managerial rights he would quickly go out of business. Chandler concludes: 'It was easy to extrapolate to a situation in which the manager regained all his old "rights" in the employment relationship while the worker moved back to the days before the Wagner Act.' (15, p. 163)

Seldom will it be possible to delegate labour relations to any such person or body external to the firm. What can always be done is to create within the firm a separate personnel department bearing sole responsibility for employer-employee relations. The danger here is that personnel may not be well integrated with other departments in the firm. Production managers may be ignorant and careless of the consequences of their decisions for labour relations, and may over-estimate the extent to which personnel officers can sort out troubles after they have occurred.

Managerial deviance

Given the nature of the industrial organization management will often be divided into rival factions over decisions about the utilization of labour and other resources. The divisions are more than a mere reflection of individual disagreements or personal antagonism; they are, rather, structural divisions inherent in the industrial enterprise. The lower levels of the hierarchy — particularly first-line supervisors — are exposed to more immediate pressures from the labour force. This can lead to a situation where foremen pursue their best interests by conniving at restrictive practices and giving unspoken recognition to workers' utilization norms. As for middle managers, they have a vested interest in the health and vigour of their own departments. Their salary, status, power, interest in the job, and self-esteem — which tend to be highly intercorrelated — may be at stake whenever decisions are taken that will have an impact on the utilization of resources.

It is not probable that managers will follow workers in the resort to collective organization to oppose unattractive decisions. Workers have less to gain by competing against one another since prospects for individual advancement are relatively slim. For most of them the surest guarantee of individual advance is collective advance. Collective organization by managers would mean alliance with rivals and would jeopardize promotion prospects, as well as violating middle-class norms of individualism. (33, p. 85) Although they may act in concert over any given issue their common interest will not be so overriding as to lead them to build a formal organization or pressure group of their own akin to a trade union. Their action will tend to be as individualized as possible and their arguments will doubtless profess a desire for efficiency.

For many purposes, then, it is fruitful to characterize the individual organization as an open system comprising varying coalitions of interested parties or stakeholders. This means the overthrow of the model of management and labour as two opposed cohesive blocs, a model that for all its crudity continues to hold sway in much that is written about industrial relations. It also leads to a revision of the view of 'organizational boundaries' as broadly coterminous with the physical boundaries of the plant. Coalitions of stakeholders, as the Chandler study reveals, can straddle these boundaries.

It is often said, of course, that the firm is an open system, a system that interacts with its environment; however, the tendency is to treat the organization's environment as if it were invariably a nuisance or a threat. This tendency can be traced to the desire, associated with self-styled functionalists, to compare social systems with natural organisms or with man-made cybernetic systems and to look for mechanisms that maintain equilibrium, or dynamic equilibrium, or even homeostasis in social systems and in society generally. A heavily used illustration of this is the blood temperature of the human body, which remains constant despite great changes in the air temperature outside, as does thermostatically controlled central heating. Here the environment is a threat, and the organism has to take defensive measures against it if it is to survive, just as the thermostat is obliged to work lest the customer complain to its manufacturer. Parallel to this process is a firm's use of inventories: stocks are built up when demand is slack and are gradually run down when demand rises. Fluctuations of demand are an annoyance since they make planning more difficult, and one way in which the firm secures itself against the vagaries of its environment is by judicious manipulation of its level of stocks. But it will not do to treat the system's environment as no more than a danger or a nuisance. The human body is crucially dependent on its environment — for food and drink, light and air. Autarky for the human body is not realizable. No more is it for the firm. Firms depend upon suppliers, retailers, customers, labour, government support and so on. More complex situations must be allowed for. One group within the enterprise may resent and another group greet intervention by 'outsiders'. In an example given earlier it was seen that the decision to employ a national firm of contractors to carry out maintenance and construction work may be supported by a contractor's association and opposed by a spokesman for the local community. Higher management may welcome the pressure brought to bear by the former and censure the unwarranted meddling of the latter; the head of the plant's maintenance department and the union organizing his men will take the opposite view. If they sense that they are losing a battle within the organization a group may deliberately appeal for 'outside' help.

The deep involvement of managers in many supposedly restrictive labour practices shows the frailty and the inadequacy of most approaches to restrictive practices. These approaches are at the same stage of development as was the study of crime before sociologists began to launch a wide-ranging and devastating attack on traditional criminology. The parallels here are worth attention. Above all, sociologists of deviance have shown that it is essential to look at the way in which acts are defined as deviant, at the processing of people through all stages of the legal apparatus, at the differential enforcement of the law, and at the processes by which laws are changed and new laws introduced. We have to repel the temptation of classifying humanity into apparently distinct categories of deviants and law-abiding citizens according to some innate and timeless quality of the acts they perform, and of proceeding to use as our master questions: in what ways are deviants different from the rest of us? and, how can they be stopped?

Whether or not any particular act is classed as deviant is a complex matter. Take the distinction between theft from a firm and the use of company materials and company time to make articles for the worker's private use ('foreigners'). (92, pp. 97-102) The distinction between outright theft and mere foreigners (the one certainly punished and the other probably not) is based on such criteria as the amount of material available and the amount required, whether the material is perceived as cheap and whether it can be obtained without the manipulation of records. As well as all this, the purported *motives* of the individual are important, for where they are deemed to be unworthy the act is far more likely to be defined as theft. Equally, manipulation of others is judged to be justified or deceitful according to the nature of the motives imputed to the actor. For example, if, during a slack period, a man used a small quantity of material that was lying around unused in order to make a birthday present for his children, this would probably count as a foreigner; if he falsified records in order to use a large quantity of scarce material to make an item for sale and went to great lengths to smuggle it out of the factory, his action would be theft and he would be sacked. Here it can be seen that effects and motives — two very different things — are used in the ascription of deviancy to an act. The effect on the company's profits will be the same whatever the use a man makes of the material and whether or not he has to resort to elaborate subterfuges to get it past the security guards at the factory gate.

Lupton's work, as outlined in chapter two, showed how foremen at 'Jay' Engineering dealt with deviant workers. For one thing, their expectations, like those of higher management, were not founded on the assumption that there would be a perfect work-flow and the fullest co-operation from workers. Instead, they looked for what Lupton calls a 'social optimum', taking into account the utilization norms of their subordinates. Social order was not imposed but *negotiated*: workers' expectations of managers helped to shape managers' behaviour and expectations. Foremen themselves had a good deal of *discretion* in dealing with workers' deviance, as did rate-fixers and time-clerks, and some 'deviant' acts were condoned or even encouraged. What counts as a restrictive practice is decided, then, not by consulting self-explanatory, universally applicable and unexceptionable edicts of managers or outside experts; rather, it emerges out of (often tacit) negotiations between workers and a wide variety of managerial officers. We have to beware, therefore, of taking managerial pronouncements about restrictive practices, which are designed for public consumption, as accurate accounts of what takes place on the shop floor.

The precise meaning and application of the term restrictive practices varies cross-culturally and historically. The term itself is, indeed, of recent origin. There was no need of it in the past, since *all* trade union activities and *all* of workers' efforts to organize collectively were treated as illegitimate. The rights of entrepreneurs over their employees were very extensive, like those of master over servant. Only gradually, and as a result of pressure exerted by liberal reformers (some of them employers), by governments, by the labour movement and by workers themselves, were labour organizations incorporated into the industrial system. Even if one believes that from a moral point of view the rights of workers are inalienable, those rights still had be asserted and won in concrete situations. Today's restrictive practice may be tomorrow's inalienable right. So it is with other forms of deviance.

Restrictive practices and the professions

'If a problem of industrial sociology is not so stated and studied that the method and findings can be applied to situations other than the industrial, it is not well stated even for industry.' (49, p. 526) So wrote the American sociologist Everett Hughes in a paper on the place of industrial sociology in the sociological enterprise generally. Elsewhere Hughes tells us that he and his associates 'became convinced that if a certain problem turned up in one occupation, it was nearly certain to turn up in all . . . The thing was to discover in what form the problem turned up, how serious it was, and how it was handled.' (49, p. 420) Significantly, this article was entitled *The Humble and the Proud* — the significance being that a large amount of Hughes's work was devoted to unearthing common features shared by humble jobs, routine manual and non-manual occupations, and esteemed bodies such as the professions. The claimed uniqueness of the proud and haughty professions was thought to be highly suspect.

So far in this book I have written of restrictive labour practices as if they were solely an aspect of relations between industrial managers on the one hand and skilled, semi-skilled and unskilled workers on the other. But what of the professions? Do they stand in splendid isolation outside the debate?

One common sociological perspective on the professions has been well described by Johnson as 'the trait approach'. (53, p. 22ff) In this perspective the uniqueness of the professions resides in their possession of a set of essential (and often interrelated) qualities or traits that are absent from or at best attenuated in ordinary run-of-the-mill occupations. The sociologist draws up a list of these traits, possibly putting them in order of importance, and is then able to measure how far any given occupation fits into the professional model. Some occupations will pass the test while others will be judged not to have made the grade owing to the absence of any or enough of the essential qualities. To draw the dividing line may be difficult, but that does not of itself invalidate the general strategy. Using the trait approach the sociologist can also examine an occupation in the process of professionalizing in order to chart and assess its progress, to identify the conditions that favour or hamper professionalism and the stages through which a successful group must pass.

'Trait theorists' have broadly agreed that professions are organized bodies whose members undergo a stipulated period of education and training to acquire skills based on theoretical knowledge. The professional association lays down and enforces strict codes of ethics, as well as testing members' competence. The professional body is geared to altruistic service to clients and to the community, and the relationship with the client is based on trust rather than suspicion, on the principle of *credat emptor* and not *caveat emptor*. Despite this broad agreement sociologists grew embarrassed at their failure to achieve complete harmony on the full list of professional traits or even on a short-list of core traits. Nor did anyone seem certain what criteria to appeal to in order to validate the decision to include or omit any suggested trait. Doubts abounded over the relations between the various traits, for sometimes one trait was taken to imply another logically, sometimes to be its cause, and sometimes to be quite unrelated to it logically or causally. Traits such as altruism were taken by some sociologists to describe the psychological motivation of individual professionals, whereas other sociologists saw altruistic service as a feature of professionalism as a social system regardless of what was taking place in the minds of particular members of the professions. Professional traits and conditions favouring the development of professionalism were also confused. Nor, finally, did it prove an easy task to hit upon acceptable operational definitions of the traits that would allow measurements to be made.

More and more groups have pretended to professional status, leading Wilensky to write a paper under the exasperated title: *The Professionalization of Everyone?* (103) Aspiring professionals have included not only the members of formerly humble associations but also people whose clients, all efforts notwithstanding, continue to view them as sharks, shysters and parasites. Sociologists, who not infrequently count themselves as professionals, may be happy enough in the company of doctors or lawyers but are less at ease when parvenus try to be their bed-fellows. One response would be to raise the qualifications for professional status, insisting on a closer observance of carefully defined codes of professional conduct. Instead of this, however, many sociologists have come to question the basis of the very distinction between professionals and the rest, recognizing that in the past they have too often taken professionals at their own roseate self-estimation. For one striking feature of the supposedly professional traits is that they are found in many occupations not normally considered professional, particularly in craft unions. Craft unions are organized bodies that insist on a period of training for apprentices, testing their competence at the end of it. They have codes of conduct embodied informally in custom and practice and formalized in the union rule-book. They are as willing as any other group to claim a technical service ideal, and baulk at outsiders without qualifications taking over their jobs. Just as professionals would not sully themselves by touting for custom through advertising so craftsmen impose similar restrictions on competition.

The problem of operationalizing professional traits shows itself very clearly in Hickson and Thomas's attempt to measure the degree of professionalism attained by a number of occupations in Great Britain. (47) Hickson and Thomas are unable to operationalize certain key elements of professionalism, namely that the professionals' skill is based on theoretical knowledge, that their service is altruistic and applied to the affairs of others, and that theirs is a non-manual occupation. Although the meaning of professionalism has thus been gutted the analysis of data proceeds. Occupations are awarded points (the 'scale item analysis coefficient') for enforcing training and examinations, for having an elaborate committee structure, for having established a monopoly, for having a Royal Charter and for the frequent publication of journals. Some of the operational definitions of professional traits are highly dubious and extremely flattering to self-styled professions. The fact that professionals provide 'an indispensable public service' is supposedly indicated by their explicit embargo on advertising, while their supplying of 'the best impartial service' is guaranteed by their refusal to undercut one another. Can it be that in this one sphere restrictions on competition are praiseworthy? And why, apart from considerations of social status, should it be thought essential that professions are non-manual?

A central assertion made on behalf of professionals is that their skill is based on theoretical knowledge. But how can the sociologist evaluate this claim, especially since, as Turner and Hodge remind us, it is bound up with the notion that the knowledge and skills of professionals can be judged only by their peers? One answer is to establish the amount of training needed to produce competent practitioners. Unfortunately, the strategy fails, for it too implies 'evaluations concerning the quality, necessity and relevance of the induction processes and training programmes'. (93, pp. 26-7) Nor could further advance be made by embracing Wilensky's proposal that when an occupation is truly professional 'preference in hiring is given to those who have proved competence to an agency external to the hiring firm or consumer'. (103, p. 138) In some cases firms and consumers have little choice owing to the establishment of a monopoly by professions (which is, anyway, one of their traits) ; and even if there is choice we still cannot be sure it will be the best one, especially if firms and consumers cannot acquire accurate information that would enable them to compare the services offered by professionals and non-professionals.

Johnson remarks sardonically that trait theorists are among the more democratic members of the sociological community in that they tend to appeal to consensus when seeking to justify their own lists of professional traits. Hickson and Thomas defend their own method and procedure on the ground that they yield 'credible' results — which means, for them, the results we should expect, with the ancient professions of the law, the clergy, the military and medicine scoring highly while less prestigeful medical ancillary occupations are among the also rans. Were this principle applied throughout sociological research it would mean the dismal conclusion that sociologists could never produce findings that were not already widely known.

A related sleight of hand is performed by Wilensky when he is confronted by the problem that since scientists do not have direct clients they cannot, on his own account, be counted as professional men and women. Nevertheless, he argues, 'the scientist's disinterested search for truth is the functional equivalent of the professional's service ideal, and where a scientific discipline has a substantial segment of its adherents fully engaged in applied work, the requisites of a profession are generally met'. (103, p. 141) He asserts without any proof or argument that a disinterested search for truth is functionally equivalent to the technical service ideal, and this device allows him to include scientists, whom he evidently admires, in the charmed circle of professionals who also win his approval.

Having realized that the professions do not possess an array of intrinsic qualities that set them apart from ordinary occupations, or having been unable or unwilling to judge the legitimacy of claims to professionalism, sociologists have turned away from trait theory. They have come instead to see professionalism not as a set of intrinsic qualities but as a particular type of occupational control, with professional ideals and self-conceptions as a body of beliefs that serve to legitimate that control. As King puts it, professional work 'is represented as making special demands upon those engaged in it . . . The distinctiveness that a profession claims for itself lies in its belief that the ideas, skills, standards and virtues it implants and cultivates in its members form a unique and inherently stable configuration.' (55, p. 69) Given this self-image professionals are charged with the mission of resisting efforts by outsiders to take over or control their work, whether the outsiders be employers, government authorities, clients, or members of other professions. Only members of his profession have any title to sit in judgment over the quality of a professional's work, and, conversely, a man has to do more than point to client satisfaction if he is to escape the accusation of quackery and charlatanism. Indeed, excessive concentration on client satisfaction will be taken as evidence of quackery. For in a professional relationship it is the producer who defines the client's needs and decides how best to deal with them. Knowledge is monopolized and the autodidact spurned.

The corpus of professional learning is expressed in an arcane language, almost impenetrable by the layman, that may or may not aid thought but that certainly protects professions against interference from outside. And although professionals have access to this specialized knowledge they also have to use a great deal of discretion in treating individual clients' problems; therefore, their work cannot be carried out by a suitably programmed automaton. The claim to combine knowledge with discretion is one typically made by occupational groups in the process of professionalizing. Skolnick shows, for example, that the assertion of professionalism made by the police force in America is bound up with their desire to ward off intervention and close scrutiny of their activities by outsiders. The appeal to professionalism 'comes to serve as an ideology undermining the capacity of police to be accountable to the rule of law', legitimating the ever-present use of discretion or justice without trial. (87, pp. 237-9)

In short, the professions display a well-developed adherence to the doctrine of vested interests, to use the Webbs' term. No one has made this point more acidly than Lees, whose view of barristers and other august professionals is that their actions 'make the London printers look like a high point of free enterprise'. (57, p.37) Echoing the Webbs, he maintains that the growth of professionalism 'means a retreat to mercantilism, and a serious brake on the emergence of new and more efficient forms of organization'; it makes life more comfortable for producers, in his opinion, but only at the expense of efficiency, vigour, diversity and idiosyncrasy. (57, pp.46-7)

Five

A Restrictive Practices Court for Labour?

In its written evidence to the Royal Commission on Trade Unions and Employers' Associations the Engineering Employers' Federation called for the establishment of an independent tribunal that would conduct public examinations of cases of alleged restrictive practices. The tribunal was to be vested with the power 'to issue an order requiring those insisting on or supporting a restrictive practice to desist therefrom'. (27, p.9) Failure to comply with an order of the court would incur legal penalties. Thus the problem of restrictive practices would be solved by a recourse to the law.

But what would be the relationship between the proposed court and the individual manager? Is it possible for any external body to legislate in detail for what should take place in negotiations at factory level? Fox argues that it is not: 'Unless the employer sees a given feature of work organization as undesirable for *him,* external denunciation gets us nowhere. It is he who administers the situation, and if he chooses to acquiesce in inefficiency then it will remain. No secret police exists or is likely to be created which can sniff out infractions of tribunal decisions on the shop floor.' (32, pp.54-5) And in the last chapter it was seen that the attitudes of managers to what are generally regarded as restrictive practices are often more ambivalent and shifting than is usually imagined.

As the restrictive practices court remains no more than a proposal it is a little difficult to present empirical evidence for or against it. One finds oneself in the limbo of the counterfactual. Nevertheless, some progress towards assessing the merits of the case can be made by looking at the effect on industrial relations of external bodies that already exist. If, for example, firms retain a substantial measure of freedom to disregard the edicts of their own employers' associations — organizations they presumably join to forward their own interests as they see them — then, one may argue, they will tend to safeguard their bargaining autonomy against invasion by complete outsiders. Since the suggestion for the tribunal came from the engineering employers it is appropriate to begin by examining the EEF itself.

In his book on labour relations in the engineering industry Marsh stresses the local, even domestic nature of negotiations. 'It is characteristic of the organization of all parties to the engineering system of industrial relations that they originated in a scattered and local fashion and have only evolved on a national scale under pressure of events.' (70, p.9) Local associations of the EEF remain conscious that it was they who preceded and founded the national organization, and they deliberately preserve their independence. In part, their localism is dictated by the varied nature of the industry, with its diversity of products, methods, and conditions — a diversity stemming from differing market demands, circumstances and techniques. Under these conditions it would be hard to formulate and enforce rigid national agreements on the way in which work should be carried out. It is by design, then, that the bulk of labour relations activity consists of negotiations between managers and workers' representatives in individual establishments. What the national agreements do is fix minimum conditions and rates, a basic structure of minima and guarantees acting as reference points in the process of wage determination at plant level. Within the basic structure each firm has scope to offer better conditions and added inducements to the work force.

The local and domestic emphasis in engineering shows itself in the handling of grievances. Far from promoting the regulation of domestic arrangements by outside bodies procedure is so fashioned as to accentuate to the full the advantages of domestic settlement. Even the last stage in procedure, the Central Conference, is not a body enunciating final solutions. Its findings are often modified largely because of the impossibility of being sure that its recommendations will be adopted on the shop floor. What is more, it is aware of 'the unwisdom of trying to force solutions which, if found difficult to apply locally or on the shop floor, in the very variable situations in which engineering establishments find themselves, might only bring its work into disrepute.' (70, pp.88-9)

Policy overtime, it was said earlier, is a means of offering inducements to labour that is often denounced by employers' associations. When asked by the Donovan Commission about their treatment of this issue representatives of the EEF replied that there was an 'understanding' among the 'club' that poaching labour was 'frowned upon'. (26, p.712) Example, persuasion, moral exhortation: these are the sanctions on which they chiefly rely. The constitutions of the federation and its local associations do provide for the expulsion of members who break agreements arrived at nationally and locally; however, since expulsion is both technically difficult and embarrassing for all concerned it rarely happens. Few firms leave the federation and still fewer are expelled. While methods of persuasion sometimes have the effect of bringing firms into line with the common policy it is clear that the ultimate sanction lacks bite. Marsh warns against the 'general tendency to overstate the control which the federation and its constituent associations exercise over member firms'. (70, p.52)

Marsh found that attitudes to poaching tended to harden if it was suspected that trade unions were trying to win wage rises in certain districts in order to use them to push up wages elsewhere ('whipsawing'). That is to say, it was only when concessions threatened to have repercussions outside the boundaries of a single firm or locality that the EEF was quick to intervene. 'Provided that issues remain purely domestic to particular establishments, other engineering employers tend to see little cause for concern.' (70, p.69) This attitude is characteristic: the federation exists for the benefit of its members, not *vice versa*, and local associations and individual employers should stay autonomous. Few of the EEF's members would admit that it does or even ought ever to enjoy substantial authority over them.

This degree of freedom in domestic negotiations is not confined to the engineering industry. For although it is common to find that employers bemoan the weakness of their organizations and deplore above all their failure to enforce decisions, it is also the case that relatively few of the critics are prepared to surrender any of their liberty in the cause of a more influential association. The Donovan Commission wryly remarked that 'the readiness of employers to federate does not . . . arise from a desire for strong organization'. (24, p.22) One of the research papers for the Commission confirmed the well-established fact that employers' associations have a limited influence on the course of industrial relations at plant level. Of those managers who had come into conflict with their association over a proposed concession to a trade union, three out of five claimed that this had made no difference to their decision. (67, pp.41-2) Allied to this is the disenchantment evinced by many about their association's effectiveness. When asked to assess the value to his firm of its membership of the British Federation of Master Printers an official of the International Publishing Corporation immediately answered that it was 'very slight indeed'. (52, p.2,619)

The EEF thought that the publicity that the activities of its suggested court would be bound to attract might embarrass unions and work groups enough to make them relinquish some of their restrictive practices. Legal penalties would be needed, however, so as to make the court really effective. Now, there is no point in equipping a body with sanctions if it is simultaneously advised not to use them. But the imposition of penalties will be likely to sour industrial relations for an employer. It is mainly for this reason that employers have been slow to exercise their right to sue workers who strike in breach of contract. Significantly, the EEF proposed that the prosecution of people refusing to abandon a restrictive practice should be brought not by the aggrieved employer but by his association. This was intended, presumably, to dissociate the employer from the legal wrangle so that none of the resulting resentment would be directed against him. It does not seem probable that this stratagem would succeed, for at the very least the employer would have to give evidence.

In her examination of cases where disputes over managerial decisions to subcontract maintenance and construction work have been taken to arbitration, Chandler attacks the supposition that 'gains' or 'losses' by management or unions are permanent. Four of the ten examples she studied had been decided in favour of the craft union, but two of the managers concerned found that their defeat had no effect on their ability to contract out the work. When a judgement has been given it 're-enters the organizational process from which it was detached' and is 'moulded and shaped by this process in the course of everyday events'. (15, p.80) It does not necessarily cease to be the subject of bargaining.

In the United States of America there are various federal and state statutes designed to outlaw some restrictive practices of labour. Prominent among these is the 'anti-featherbedding' clause of the Taft-Hartley Act, which deems it unfair labour practice for a union 'to cause or attempt to cause an employer to pay or deliver or agree to pay or deliver any money or other thing of value, in the nature of an exaction, for services which are not performed or not to be performed'. Various decisions by the Supreme Court have, however, made this proscription useless. The Court did not prevent the International Typographical Union from insisting on 'bogus work' (needless repetition), nor was a prohibition issued against the American Federation of Musicians when it compelled a theatre to pay local performers to stand by during a concert given by a nationally famous band. (78, p.145) Such examples make it clear that the Supreme Court has taken so narrow a view of what constitutes services not performed or not to be performed that a union would have to blunder seriously in order to fall foul of the Act.

Granted, the 'anti-featherbedding' clause is at such a high degree of generality that everything depends on the Supreme Court's interpretation of it. As with the American constitution the Supreme Court has a legislative as well as a purely judicial role: it does not simply enforce the law, but has to interpret it so much that it is in effect deciding by its own lights the merits of the cases brought before it. One might argue, therefore, that it would be wiser to frame a law that gave a detailed list of practices considered to be restrictive. This would ignore the problem that each practice might be restrictive in one context, protective in another and of advantage to all sides in a third — the range of possible contexts being infinite. An impossible burden would be given to any court or tribunal that was set up. Taft himself saw this. In defence of the legislation bearing his name he argued that it was 'impractical to give to a board or a court the power to say that so many men are all right and so many men are too many. It would require a practical application of the law by the courts in hundreds of different industries, and a determination of facts which it seemed . . . would be almost impossible.' (78, p.145)

Underlying the case in favour of a restrictive practices court for labour is the assumption that it would take an uncompromising line in dealing with restrictive practices. Having determined by an impartial, objective inquiry that a given practice was restrictive it would simply declare that the employer, union or work group should abandon it.

The suspicion must be voiced that courts would not always behave in this way. Take, for example, the findings and recommendations of a court of inquiry, chaired by Lord Cameron, that looked into problems arising from the introduction of web-offset presses into two printing houses. (13) In both cases there had been a dispute between the unions and management over the question, how many men were needed to operate the new machines? Naturally enough, the unions' calculation of the number of men required was higher than that of management. To this problem the court thought that it had a straightforward answer: it proclaimed the need for an objective study of the manning question and chided all concerned for their failure to suggest that this be done. And while accepting that a national agreement on manning scales was not feasible it insisted that there should be a national agreement on *methods* of arriving at manning levels in individual cases.

The attendant jurisdictional conflicts were, however, less tractable. At Southwark Offset the company had agreed in consultation with the unions that machine minders should make the fullest possible use of assistants, and that a system of 'pool-manning' should be started. The IPC and the non-craft union SOGAT took this to mean that *all* the staff on each shift could be interchanged as the need arose; but the craft unions — the National Graphical Association and the Amalgamated Society of Lithographic Printers — intended pool-manning to mean no more than that minder should be interchangeable with minder and assistant with assistant. The craft preserve could not be bought so cheaply.

At the Co-operative Press, Manchester, SOGAT claimed that since web-offset lithographic printing was a completely new process the existing national agreement on sheet-fed lithographic presses (under which SOGAT members performed only the less skilled operations) was inappropriate. In its stead the union brought forward two proposals: either SOGAT members should take on the duties they already had on rotary letterpress machines or web-offset should be manned by an integrated staff drawn from all three unions. Both suggestions would have involved a great deal of encroachment on the craft domains of the NGA and the ASLP. These two unions rejected the proposals outright.

Web-offset is a hybrid process demanding two different kinds of experience and expertise. On the one hand it displays most of the mechanical features of web-fed letterpress machines, which were the province of the NGA and SOGAT; on the other hand its technical characteristics are those of sheet-fed lithographic presses, which were operated by members of the ASLP in conjunction with SOGAT assistants. Judging by technical competence alone, then, all three unions could plausibly claim that their members had the knowledge and experience demanded. There was no clear-cut case in favour of any one of them.

The Cameron Inquiry realized that to discuss the problem solely in these terms, to venture to determine objectively which union was best qualified to lay claim to the work done on web-offset presses, would not strike at the heart of the problem. For beneath the argument about technical knowledge and experience lay an intestine struggle in the printing industry between craft and non-craft unions. The former were rigidly opposed to an invasion of the craft domain. As for SOGAT, it was patently worried about the lack of avenues to promotion for its men, and had seized on the chance provided by the development of the web-offset process of printing. The tendency of the printing unions to polarize into craft and non-craft blocs has been marked ever since the Second World War, and when the ASLP merged with the NGA and Natsopa amalgamated with the NUPB & PW to form SOGAT it looked as if the process had been almost completed, until SOGAT split apart again through internal dissension.

Under these circumstances the Cameron Inquiry recommended in effect a return to the previous frontiers, to the *status quo ante bellum.* It upheld the claims of the craft unions largely in the hope that this judgement would do least to endanger the possibility of an amalgamation of SOGAT with the NGA and an eventual withering away of artificial and restrictive craft barriers. *The court was taking the line of least resistance on union jurisdiction.* A deep clash of values, traditions and interests is not settled so easily or in the same way as is a less highly charged conflict over manning levels, though this too can be troublesome enough. The court appreciated that ultimately the problem could be solved only by some arrangement mutually agreed by the unions concerned with the support of their members.

Another Court of Inquiry took the line of least resistance when it investigated a demarcation dispute at a steel works in Corby. The Engineers claimed that the machining of 'hollows' ought to be done by their members, whereas the British Iron, Steel and Kindred Trades' Association pointed out that custom and practice at the factory restricted engineers to maintenance work only. The company itself had put forward the compromise that the work be shared between the unions. This, the court held, would have exacerbated the conflict. Since the work was not maintenance it should not be done by the engineers. The court upheld custom and practice not because this produced the most efficient organization of production but simply out of a desire to minimize unrest and keep the peace. (19, p. 67)

Instead of acting as a surrogate management eager to exercise its rights, external bodies have sometimes acknowledged, tacitly or openly, that problems of resource utilization need to be treated in such a way as to gain the consent of the workers concerned. This would require wholly different approaches, of the kind discussed in the following chapter.

Six

Productivity Bargaining and Industrial Democracy

The attraction and feasibility of productivity bargains

Why is the phrase 'restrictive practices' pejorative? Why are restrictive practices judged to be unjustified? — Not because it is thought that an employer buys a man's labour in the same way as he buys capital equipment. Although that analogy may have been drawn in the past, few people in advanced societies would now argue that agreement on a contract of employment means that the employer can assume the right unilaterally to determine the ways in which labour is to be deployed and disciplined. His employees are not in that sense his property. Rather, restrictive practices are considered to be detrimental in so far as they lead to the wasteful utilization of labour and equipment.

Barriers to efficiency are not the same thing as invasions of so-called managerial rights. Attempts by unions or work groups to regulate the area of managerial relations by asserting their own utilization norms do not necessarily limit efficiency and may even promote it. Moreover, it is a mistake to assume that all obstacles to the efficient organization of production are raised officially or unofficially by labour. Some have their origin in management itself or at any rate receive tacit support from managers. Wasteful labour utilization may be caused by managers' incompetence. More than this, managers as well as workers may be stakeholders in what at least appear to be wasteful practices. There are also cases where the position of a particular manager in the power structure of his firm is such that he has a stake in a practice which some or all of his colleagues are trying to remove.

Some writers on industrial relations have shied away from speaking of restrictive practices and have focussed instead on a seemingly more important and unambiguous term: *waste*. They argue that there is now a mounting pile of undeniable evidence that resources in industry are frequently squandered. Fox remarked that management consultants have believed British industry to be employing some ten or 15 per cent more manpower than is required by existing processes, and that in many cases a 40 per cent saving in manpower is feasible. A report of the Iron and Steel Board found that 'the output required from British steel works could be achieved by a considerably smaller labour force than at present'. (32, p.52) A study by the Chemical Economic Development Committee argued that changes in attitudes and practices could, on their own and without any other reforms, produce a manpower saving in the industry that 'could well be as much as 20 per cent of the present numbers employed; alternatively it could take the form of a 25 per cent increase in output from the existing employee force'. (24, p.75) Most dramatic, perhaps, was the finding of the Shawcross Commission that the four national newspapers it investigated were overmanned by 53 per cent in their production and distribution departments. (85, p.210) Flanders' study of the productivity agreements negotiated by Esso at Fawley purported to show that these estimates of waste in industry were far from exaggerated. The first of the agreements, on Flanders' appraisal, accounted for a rise in productivity per man hour of 50 per cent in two years. (30, pp.192-3) More evidence of what could be achieved was provided by the 1960 longshore mechanization agreement for the west coast of the United States. Hartman estimated that after decades of stagnation productivity rose by around 40 per cent between 1960 and 1965. (44, p.127) Most of this increase was attributed directly to the mechanization agreement; and while the profit position of the Pacific coast companies improved steadily from 1960 onwards, that of the Atlantic companies, which had no similar agreement, suffered a decline. (44, pp.176-7)

One approach to the problem of waste that would appeal to

a good many sociologists would be to isolate certain structural variables — technology of production, nature of product markets, cost structure of the firm, methods of payment, workers' prior orientations, union structures, attitudes of union leaders and so on — and relate these causally to one another and to the extent of waste in different industries. This is the programme Lupton carried out in *On the Shop Floor*. The ability of managers at 'Jay' Engineering Company to tolerate output restriction and the manipulation of the piecework system was explained in terms of the firm's cost structure and the nature of the market in which it operated. The market was stable (partly because of restrictive trading practices) and labour costs were small in relation to total costs. This meant that there was little downward pressure on earnings. Limits to competition between firms had made life cosier, and rises in labour costs would not greatly affect 'Jay's' prices and thereby the demand for its product. In contrast, the market for the clothes produced by 'Wye' Garments approached more closely the model of perfect competition, with a large number of small firms and an absence of cartelization. For this firm the ratio of labour costs to total costs was high. Increased labour costs would have been a serious threat to 'Wye's' profitability. In these circumstances it would have been nearly impossible for managers to tolerate the kind of 'fiddles' allowed at 'Jay', since the pressure to keep wage costs as low as they could was very great. Trade unions and the shop steward system were in any case poorly developed, so that managers did not have to deal with 'the challenge from below'. (64, pp.195-6)

Managers are often known to argue that certain factors make them more vulnerable than their counterparts in other industries to practices that hamstring the efficient deployment of resources. Newspaper publishers, for example, tend to maintain that 'newspapers are different' — Shawcross called this dismissively 'the traditional management defence'. (85, p. 40) The character of a daily newspaper and its contents are transient: it is impossible to make up a day's stoppage since yesterday's paper holds diminished delights. A prolonged stoppage of work could lead customers to switch permanently to a rival paper and could mean kissing goodbye to future advertising revenue. Managers, in short, are forced to give in to inefficiency: they are not masters of their fate. Northrup gives similar reasons for wasteful labour utilization in the supermarket industry in America: stocks are perishable and the goodwill of customers strictly provisional.

It would be foolish to repudiate these excuses completely, for there are good reasons to believe that exploration of the relationship between structural factors of the kind outlined above and the amount of waste in any given sector would be fruitful. Advocates of productivity bargaining do not deny this, though they have done little themselves to examine waste from this standpoint. Probably they are afraid of putting convenient excuses into the hands of managers, who are inclined to engage in special pleading to explain their connivance at practices they profess to deplore. It is all too easy to think of the arguments they could draw on to exonerate themselves: we cannot risk losing the goodwill of our customers; our stocks are perishable; we must meet vital export orders; production in our plant is easily disrupted; the cost to us of breakdowns in production is crippling; multi-unionism bedevils negotiations on the revision of work practices; other firms capitulate and we have to follow suit.

One underlying message of Flanders' influential book on Fawley was that these structural factors should not be blown up into ready-made justifications of wasteful practices. According to Flanders the barriers to higher productivity were not so much external, given and unalterable as self-imposed. He denounced the passive contentment of British managers to await initiatives from unions, their failures of self-confidence, their enslavement to empty exhortation and propaganda, and, lying behind all this, their avoidance of tough negotiations in search of a quiet life. Weakness of will, laziness, ignorance and lack of vision were the ills to be treated first. The cure? — A programme of education, enlightenment and encouragment, to which Flanders himself made a powerful contribution. As the movement gained strength the example of successful productivity bargains struck by pioneering firms would encourage the others.

This message was picked up and retransmitted by the authors of a paper on the reform of collective bargaining

written on behalf of the Department of Employment.
Reporting on the experience with productivity bargains of
eleven companies they drew a happy conclusion. All the firms
ach eved beneficial reforms with the unions' blessing, and
defects were put right and procedural and substantive changes
introduced in accordance with the thrust of the Donovan
Report. Big improvements in economic performance were
made. But these were not exceptional companies in terms of
size or management structure or union development or market
situation or technology. What made them exceptional was 'the
extent to which they believed that properly planned initiatives
could result in real improvements in their situation. Where
they managed to lead, others might well be expected to
follow'. (21, p.86)

The message, was, in fact, already present in a
memorandum prepared for Esso in 1958 by an American firm
of efficiency consultants. It was this memorandum that
sparked off the negotiations at Fawley. Would the plans for
change be opposed within Esso itself as well as by rival oil
companies, by other industries and by left- and right-wing
trade unions? Perhaps so, but no matter, for then 'it would
have to be explained to these groups that Esso's decision to
adopt this policy is based on the soundest financial and human
considerations, and that any other group could, therefore,
adopt the same policy if it wished to do so'. (30, p. 264) This,
for Flanders, was the memorandum's 'most daring premise'.
(30, p. 81) Esso's opponents and detractors would have to be
brought face to face with their own failings and
responsibilities.

The scope of productivity bargaining
To understand what sort of agreements Flanders was calling
for it is helpful to look at a criticism that misses the mark but
that has been repeated often. The negotiations at Fawley
supposedly embody 'the buy-out approach' to restrictive
practices, an approach that is self-stultifying: 'the perverse
psychology of the buy-out means that continued use of this
approach will not work. It is all too easy for the idea, "bad
practices are a good thing since they command a price", to
pervert the sense of accomplishment throughout an

organization.' (84, p.17) Workers will be encouraged cynically to hoard new restrictive practices in order to offer them for sale in the future: 'People learn that their loose practices are worth money. This is an invitation for them to develop other bad practices in readiness for the next negotiation.' (84, p.4) As one restrictive practice is uprooted so a new one sprouts to replace it.

Schultz and McKersie go on to distinguish two types of buy-out productivity bargain. One is the piecemeal approach of Esso at Fawley, the other 'a general buy-out for an overall price'. As an example of the second they refer to the agreement reached in 1960 between the Pacific Maritime Association and the International Longshoremen's and Warehousemen's Union, an agreement that lead to the thoroughgoing modernization of work rules and practices in the west coast longshoring industry. For Schultz and McKersie this was a straightforward affair requiring the answer to one simple question asked by the employers: 'What will it cost us to have a free hand to do away with these (restrictive) practices?' The price proved to be ten million dollars, to be paid in five annual instalments into a fund that would act as security for the promise that hours of work per week should not fall below thirty-five, with an average of forty. The Pacific Maritime Association also agreed to put fifteen million dollars in five annual instalments into a pension fund. In return, the employer was to have the right to revise any rule or practice provided he could demonstrate, first, that the revision could not be avoided if he were to operate efficiently, change methods of work or introduce labour-saving devices, and, second, that it would neither put an onerous work-load on the individual worker nor create unsafe conditions. Summarizing the agreement Killingsworth says that the employers 'simply "bought out" the contractual rules which required the employment of unnecessary men'. (54, p.305)

The Mechanization and Modernisation Agreement was not, however, so simple. The initiative came from a policy decision of the union involved — the ILWU — and the problems were debated at many union caucuses. This helped to convince the rank-and-file that other forms of protection could be exchanged for the old work practices without a sacrifice of security. The attempt to persuade their members that a relaxation of their customary practices would be advantageous was initiated by the union's leaders in 1957, a full three years before the settlement was concluded, and continued even after this. The problems involved were discussed at union meetings, proposals were circulated in printed form and voted on in a coast-wide referendum. One of the union's negotiators has claimed that: 'Without such an educational process, the men would never have been willing to change working conditions which they had fought for originally and had enjoyed for years.' (22, p.92) It is worth noting, too, that the union had firm control over the dockers owing to the influence of the union hiring-hall: an illustration of the importance of the 'internal strength' of trade unions.

The likely result of treating productivity bargaining as a simple buy-out can be seen from the example of the steel strike in the United States. In July of 1959 a nation-wide strike began in the American steel industry when the old contracts of work had expired. The union's demands, presented as soon as negotiations opened, were conventional by American standards. They called for wage increases, shorter hours of work, higher pensions and supplementary employment benefits, improvements in the insurance scheme, a union shop, additional paid holidays and the streamlining of grievance procedures. Just before the outbreak of the strike the steel companies had raised the problem of local working rules (clause 2B) which, they alleged, hindered all efforts to maximize efficiency. Management's power to decide on crew sizes, rest periods, arrangements for the replacement of workers and on other working conditions had been circumscribed by several clauses in the old contracts. Therefore, managers claimed, any offer of wage rises and other economic benefits could only be considered when the union acknowledged the right of management to assert its authority by eliminating those restrictive practices embodied in local working rules. Three months later the companies declared themselves willing to submit the whole question to arbitration. The whole question was: 'What, if any, changes should be made in the local working conditions to enable the companies to take reasonable steps to improve efficiency and eliminate waste with due regard to the welfare of the employees?' (51, p.65n) The effect on workers of the companies' forthright bid to reclaim managerial rights by buying-out local working rules has been described thus: 'What had been a half-hearted, desultory strike on the part of the workers at once became a militant, determined contest. At stake was not the preservation of old work rules keyed to an alleged archaic technology, but the workers' rights to "due process" in any revision of their rules. Featherbedding had never been an aggravated problem in the steel mills. However, the impatience of the engineers with "due process" snatched defeat out of the jaws for victory for the companies.' (43, p.117)

There was more to productivity bargaining, for Flanders, than merely buying restrictive practices. One point he emphasized repeatedly was that productivity bargaining heightened the consciousness of managers and workers, leading them to recognise waste where previously they had not seen it. In a similar vein, Zweig wrote that some firms 'may have adapted themselves so well to (a) practice that they do not feel it at all or do not realize its existence'. He adds: 'It is interesting to recall here that my first respondent among employers in the cotton industry told me emphatically that he does not know of any restrictive practices in his mills, either on spinning or weaving.' (105, p.19) McCarthy and Parker's survey discovered the same self-confidence among those interviewed. Sixty per cent of the works managers and 49 per cent of the personnel officers said that there were no time-wasting or inefficient labour practices in their establishments. (67, p.93) These claims, even if sincere, have been questioned. They often reflect, argues Fox, the weak aspirations of management towards efficiency of manpower utilization — that is, they have set themselves low standards. (33, p.171)

In recent years industrial relations experts have pointed to systematic overtime as a widespread source of waste in industry — although it is possible that they have overstated the case. (95, pp.354-5) One of the reasons why systematic overtime has been so often neglected is that it does not conform to the accepted view of what restrictive practices are.

Above all, it has nothing to do with union rules. The official pronouncements of union leaders condemn the use of overtime to offer inducements to labour and to provide an adequate wage packet. Employers' associations could scarcely fail to agree. The trouble is that neither are trade unions in a position actively to enforce a policy that would mean less money for their members, nor do employers' associations have the power and determination to dictate behaviour to federated firms. Systematic overtime is a workplace institution. The usual level of overtime worked in the factory comes to be accepted as right and proper by managers and workers alike. Just as workers would resist attempts to reduce overtime hours so managers would complain about any general refusal to put in extra hours (an overtime ban). When a practice fails to fit the received idea of restrictive practices it may not count as wasteful. Where there are no obvious culprits whose malice, subversive ideals, laziness, irrationality or incompetence can be blamed for wasteful practices the waste itself is often unnoticed. And where managers and workers have a zero-sum approach to bargaining — where, that is to say, each party to the negotiations believes that a gain by one side is automatically a loss by the other — then, Shepard has observed, the negotiators are blind to interests held in common and tend to misrepresent each other's bargaining position. So there is a self-imposed impasse: opportunities are not seized because they are only dimly perceived. The upshot is that the losers never feel that justice has been done, whereas the winners are trapped into relying on the same methods that won for them in the past: 'Questioning of the structure that produced victory is psychologically impossible.' (86, pp.132-3)

Productivity bargaining is supposed to point the way out of the zero-sum, wins-losses morass. Thus the Prices and Incomes Board noted that the planning of a productivity agreement 'already had an effect by inducing cost-consciousness, by providing new information about performance and new methods of assessing performance, and by directing attention to the possibility of changing methods of work'. (77, p.25) Esso's evidence to Donovan struck up the same theme: 'Our experience is that there is a tremendous fund of interest in, and knowledge of, work practice throughout an organization, which it is the task of management to release and use'; this task meant 'a considerable revision of ideas about "management prerogative" '. (28, p. 1,653)

Consent and the social contract

Where changes in managerial attitudes have happened, many would argue, they have not arisen from nowhere nor have they been simply a soul-searching response to clarion calls from academic industrial relations experts. Direct pressure from workers has been a powerful stimulus — a product of full employment and economic growth in the post-war period. The pressure has been not only on wages but also for the greater incorporation of workers into the process of decision-making, which will require changes in the structure of collective bargaining and changes in attitudes.

Consider, for example, the implications of Zweig's remark that most employers are convinced that 'the restrictive spirit' causes more harm than do restrictive rules. One might ask: what is the meaning of this platitude? What does it matter if workers are sullen, if the restrictive spirit is part of their outlook on life, provided they abide by the terms and conditions of their contracts of employment? — Zweig goes on to provide the answer: 'every legitimate and commonly agreed practice can become restrictive if the restrictive spirit is infused into it'; indeed, 'no practice is conceivable which cannot be misapplied if one side wishes to do so'. (105, p.24) A formally agreed contract, whose provisions cannot normally be precise and detailed, is no better than useless if it does not enjoy a measure of genuine support from the work force. For the sanctions available to workers have such strength and can assume so many forms that any agreement can be made worthless. In any case, far from being the *summum bonum*, rigid adherence to formally agreed rules is one of the most widely publicized types of pressure that workers and unions can exert. If absolute power is impossible there is no substitute for goodwill. In the case of the port transport industry, for instance, where the port employers had aimed at more realistic manning standards and better time-keeping in exchange for decasualization, Devlin pointed out that although they could easily get an acknowledgement of the general need to agree on stricter manning levels the agreement would be vacuous if it could not be applied to actual cases, where notions of 'realism' would be bound to differ. The employers could insert a clause promising better time-keeping, but they already had many such clauses. 'What they need', Devlin concluded, 'is not a fresh repetition of an old promise but a new atmosphere in which they can secure the observance of the agreements they have already got.' (22, p.120)

This need to gain workers' consent was stressed in Behrend's discussion of piecework systems of payment. She attacked people who believe — as many do — that the essence of an incentive scheme is the scientific, objective, dispassionate determination of a fair day's work and a fair day's pay by job evaluation and work study techniques. It is often conceded, of course, that such schemes work better with 'consultation' than without it: but the consultation, which is usually empty and ineffective ritual, is seen as merely an initial application of oil to help the machine to function. Behrend argued, in contrast, that a successful incentive scheme *consists of* agreement on norms: through a process of 'effort bargaining' the idea is accepted that standards of effort on piecework ought to be higher than on time work. 'The critical factor', she wrote, 'is the worker's attitude to incentives and his willingness to increase his level of effort, and this must depend on the existence of mutual consultation and agreement.' (5, p.505) Similarly, both Roy and Lupton demonstrated that when workers consider a particular rate to be too tight they either try to cheat or else adopt deliberately unco-operative tactics so that it will be changed in their favour. Rate-fixers are not so much scientists as diplomats.

Productivity bargaining is not, then, a one-off exercise but a continuing process that marks a new style of employment relationship based on the consent of the work force. The new dispensation is described in McCarthy and Ellis's *Management by Agreement*, a work that stands in direct line of descent from Flanders' study of Fawley and from Fox's theoretical discussion of power and authority in industry. The core of management by agreement is that 'authority must be shared with workers through an extension of the area of joint regulation'. (68, p.96) Now, all this emphasis on the importance of consent to authority points to one thing: the revival of social contract theory in the literature of industrial relations.

Social contract theory has had to face a number of problems: When has an individual given his consent to government? What does he have to do to withdraw it? Is consent different from enforced obedience or grudging **acquiescence?** Does consent have to be well-informed, or can it be the ill-informed outcome of ignorance or the short-sighted result of false consciousness? — Some of these problems are made still more difficult by the changed social context in which the social contract is being asked to operate. For social contract theory, as Partridge argues, grew up in the context of an individualist outlook on society. The individual's relations with the state were seen to be direct rather than mediated through voluntary associations and pressure groups. Further-more, the legitimate functions of the state were severely limited and centred round the provision of protection and security to lives and property. When we try to apply social contract theory to the relations between employer and employed in modern industry we confront added problems. For one thing, these relations are not direct and unmediated, and it would be foolish to ignore the role of trade unions and less formalized work groups. Again, we are not dealing with consent in a static society where the role of the state is minimal. Many industries are characterized by rapid technological and organizational change, and this is not so much a nuisance to them as a part of their very being. Management plays an active part in the life of workers as does the state in the wider society. Partridge indicates one consequence of this: ' a government that is always disturbing and modifying existing arrangements of activities, relation-ships and rights must find more trouble in retaining the consent of the governed than the relatively "inactive" or conservative governments that individualistic, natural-right theorists such as Locke had in mind'. (79, p.25)

The willingness to struggle to gain workers' consent has been linked by Fox to the pluralist, as distinct from the unitary, perspective on the employment relationship. The unitary view emphasizes the common objectives, common interests and shared values of managers and workers. There is a unified loyalty and authority structure within which managerial rights are legitimized by all. Conflict is undesirable and trade unions, being sectional and potentially disruptive forces, are accepted only suspiciously if at all. Liberal use of 'team' and 'family' metaphors is made by people who have a unitary frame of reference. They see it as quite in order for employers to assert their rights over employees by the use of power and with the direct aid, when necessary, of legal sanctions against the (tiny minority of) dissidents. The pluralist view is very different from this. Pluralists acknowledge that an industrial enterprise contains groups with competing claims and rival interests, so that conflict, within limits, is not necessarily a sign of industrial ill-health — quite the reverse, in fact. Trade unions and unofficial work groups have a rightful part to play in the running of the enterprise: they are neither historical survivals from an inhumane and harsh industrial past, nor are they simply power bases for political subversives, nor yet are they irrational and misguided sectional groups undermining the firm's or the national interest. (34)

The choice between these two frames of reference has important consequences, Fox argues, for the conduct of industrial relations locally and nationally. One aspect of this is that people who adopt a unitary view of the industrial enterprise tend to have a blinkered and excessively legalistic approach to the question: when has consent been given? In their view consent may be implied 'simply by accepting the employment contract, or by signing for a copy of company rules, or by being covered by a collective agreement concluded with a trade union, or even, perhaps, by being subjects of a political regime that has enacted certain legislation by "democratic" processes'. (34, p. 189) Inspired by a unitary ideology the short-lived Industrial Relations Act betrayed ' a total lack of interest in the practical mechanics of winning consent from the governed'. (34, p.201) The 'consent' that is spoken of by people who have the unitary perspective can be, then, a very feeble thing. When there is industrial conflict a unitary view encourages us to say that workers acknowledge the legitimacy of the norms they are defying, so that their action is a breach of promise, a violation of voluntarily entered contractual obligations.

Pluralists, in contrast, treat the giving of consent in a less cavalier fashion, since they are far more sensitive to the distinction between active consent and passive acquiescence. What pluralists want are regularized institutional arrangements that will allow workers legitimately to pursue their own interests. 'Informal' understandings between managers and workers are no substitute for this: far from being a sign of healthy co-operation and mutual confidence, the widespread reliance on informal dealings has been attacked by pluralists as the product of reciprocated mistrust, of fond attachment to a flexibility that is usually spurious, and of fear of reprisals for departing from the doctrine of managerial rights. (66, pp.27-8) In their writings on productivity bargaining pluralists have underlined time and again the need for managers to ensure that the workers concerned have been properly consulted and adequately represented in negotiations. When this is not done, they argue, workers cannot truly be said to have consented to the productivity package and delays and unrest can be confidently expected. Thus the Prices and Incomes Board noted that a productivity deal at ICI was seriously delayed mainly because 'the first occasion on which local managers, shop stewards and employees received definite information about the proposals was when the agreement, already signed, was distributed to them'. (77, p.33) In an otherwise broadly optimistic report on the reform of collective bargaining the Department of Employment found that in many firms managers and workers were poorly prepared for the changes, and that misunderstandings were frequent. On the part of management there was a general failure to appreciate the new problems that unions would be bound to face — the added burden on lay officials, for example. Most surprising was that 'distribution of the agreements was generally very limited, and in some cases it was not even thought necessary to issue copies to shop stewards'. (21, p.69)

When to decide that consent has been granted is an old and troublesome problem for social contract theory. John Locke gave one answer in a famous passage in his Second Treatise of Civil Government: 'Every man that hath any possession or enjoyment of any part of the dominions of any government doth thereby give his tacit consent, and is as far forth obliged to obedience to the laws of that government during such enjoyment as any one under it; whether this his possession be of land to him and his heirs for ever, or a lodging only for a week; or whether it be barely travelling freely on the highway; and in effect it reaches as far as the very being of any one within the territories of the government.' Progressively the criteria become more lax, so that in the end a person only has to stand on the ground in a country to have given his consent to the regime. Consent such as this is, obviously, not always eager and wholehearted. Locke adds the harsh assurance that if a man wants to withdraw his consent from the government 'he is at liberty to go and incorporate himself into any other commonwealth, or to agree with others to begin a new one, *in vacuis locis,* in any part of the world they can find free and unpossessed'. (59, pp.60-1) It is precisely this formalistic attitude to consent that pluralist commentators on industrial relations have attacked. Furthermore, in the modern industrial enterprise existing activities, expectations, rights and obligations are for ever changing, and incessant social change means that the social contract has to be renewed continually if it is to be a true expression of consent to government. Recognizing this, pluralists have stressed that winning consent is a difficult and a continuing battle.

In their eagerness to see that there are institutionalized checks to power ensuring that trade unions are an effective opposition to managerial rule, pluralists have been inclined to worry less about the achievement of internal democracy within unions themselves. They have been too unconcerned with 'the Michels problem', namely that as organizations grow in size they develop, because of social and psychological forces, an entrenched and self-perpetuating ruling oligarchy that acts as a barrier to democratic processes in the organization even if that organization is officially committed, as trade unions are, to democratic participation in decision-making. (74) In Clegg's *A New Approach to Industrial Democracy,* the emphasis is on the 'countervailing power' of trade unions rather than on their internal structure, and the apathy and non-participation of the rank-and-file is not felt as a besetting problem. Clegg sees an organized and effective opposition to managerial rule — a permanent opposition that should never become the government of industry — as the embodiment of democracy. Having stated flatly that it is irrelevant whether the means of production are in private hands or are collectively owned Clegg propounds two basic principles necessary to democracy in industry: first, unions must be independent of the state and of management so that they are not merely puppet organizations, and, second, they must be the sole representatives of workers' interests so that managers would not be able to set up rival bodies such as consultative committees that would sap the unions' strength. (18, pp.21ff) Dislike of unilateral rule and managerial diktat pervade the book, but participation in decision-making is quietly dropped as a defining characteristic of democracy.

In a more recent book in the same tradition, McCarthy and Ellis defend trade unions against critics who seize on 'those features of trade unionism that seem to outsiders to exemplify undemocratic and anti-social attitudes towards other workers — namely the enforcement of the closed shop, inadequacies of union rule books that permit unfair elections and other malpractices, and the effects on individuals of certain kinds of restrictive practices'. (68, p.17) If unions are to be a powerful opposition they have to remain united and they must have sanctions to impose on dissident individuals — and while the unions' critics may deplore curtailments of individual liberty they often exhort unions to discipline their members lest industrial anarchy break out. There is a conflict of values here — the freedom of the individual versus effective counter-weights to unilateral rule — and compromises have to be made. Characteristically, the pluralist writers go too far in their defence of collective organization; for whatever one may say about the closed shop and restrictive practices it is surely incontestable that the rigging of elections does not merely seem undemocratic: it is undemocratic. This brings us back to the point made earlier, that social contract theory was meant to describe the direct relations between the individual and the state. In most industries in democratic countries today the relations between worker and manager are mediated through unions; and for the social contract to operate it is essential that unions be so organized as to reflect the opinions of their members accurately. Not just managerial attitudes but also trade union structure and organization can stand in the way of the kind of employment relationship — management by agreement — that McCarthy and Ellis are calling for.

Power and authority

The fullest and most subtle application of social contract theory to industrial relations has been made by a sociologist, Alan Fox. Crucial to his analysis is the distinction he draws between power and authority, which is in turn linked to the distinction between unitary and pluralist perspectives: for the unitary view is associated with unbending assertions of managerial rights and the use of power to discipline recalcitrants, whereas the pluralist perspective encourages authority relationships based on consent.

Fox's discussion of power and authority draws on Buckley's *Sociology and Modern Systems Theory* but ultimately diverges from it. Power, for Buckley, consists of the direct or indirect control of the behaviour of other people against their will or without their informed commitment and understanding. Similar control, but now with the informed and committed consent of subordinates, is what makes up authority. Consent is thought to be 'something socially and psychologically deeper than mere acquiescence or overt compliance', and to decide in a given case whether or not a set of social norms or institutions has taken on the legitimacy that is conferred by informed consent would require 'a good deal of knowledge on the level of social-psychological dynamics', because the fact that subordinates comply with the exercise of control does not mean necessarily that they have consented to the control. Informed voluntary compliance is, Buckley says, 'a definite psychological state'. (12, pp.177-186)

Fox's account of power and authority deviates from Buckley's in one important way. Having, as Buckley does, defined authority in terms of consent, Fox points out that 'this does not exclude the possibility that (an individual's) consent may have been secured by the use of pretence or deception which leaves him ignorant of certain facts, implications, or probable consequences. The pejorative use of the term "manipulation" covers these cases, though manipulation is sometimes seen as a separate method of controlling behaviour'.

(33, p.35n) The problem this raises — the difference between informed and uninformed consent, authority and manipulation — is not dealt with at all squarely by Buckley. All he has to say, indeed, is the statement already quoted, that informed voluntary compliance is a distinct, unique state of mind. It is admittedly true that when people give their consent to social arrangements there are many who are half- or even fully aware that they are not well-informed. This will give their consent a reserved, tentative and above all provisional quality that will not taint the response of anyone who thinks he is fully informed. Someone in this second position may well have a special outlook: sure, confident, committed. However, while it may be true that a person who *believes* himself to be the possessor of accurate information is in a different frame of mind from someone whose consent is confessedly blind, this does not tell us whether the former man's belief is in fact *correct*. He may be mistaken or deceiving himself.

One way out is to duck the problem. We could simply say that it makes no difference whether or not people are fully informed, adding that it would be difficult or impossible to decide what counted as full information. All that matters, it could be said, is that consent is willing rather than reluctant, active rather than dull. Now, a vital part of Fox's case is to argue against this way of tackling the problem. First, he points to the potentially disruptive effect of subordinates' realization that they have been uninformed or misinformed. Authority won by manipulative tactics 'lasts only as long as the subordinate remains ignorant, and his discovery of them is likely to modify sharply his frame of reference towards management's legitimacy for some time into the future'. (33, p.35n) The ill-feeling will be particularly acute where managers have set out deliberately to deceive. Manipulation is a risky affair because if the truth gets abroad the edifice of authority will collapse. Informed consent is more stable than uninformed consent, however enthusiastic the latter may be. There is more to it than this, however, as Fox makes clear elsewhere. That a social system be geared to generate *informed* consent is taken by him to be a good thing in itself quite apart from questions of expediency; it represents 'an attempt to grapple with the full implications of increasing literacy, growing insistence on the citizen's right to formulate his own beliefs and aspirations in the light of the facts available, and a diminishing disposition to define conventions as unchangeable laws'. (34, p.226) The battle will be hard, given 'the high degree of acceptance of the *status quo* which is such a marked feature of our society'. (34, p.216)

A parallel to Fox's discussion of informed and uninformed consent can be found in the writings of John Stuart Mill. What do we make of cases where someone holds opinions we know or believe to be correct but where he has no grasp of the foundation of his opinions and could not offer a reasoned defence of them? For one thing, says Mill, the situation is extremely fragile, since 'to shut out discussion entirely is seldom possible, and when it once gets in, beliefs not grounded on conviction are apt to give way before the slightest semblance of an argument'. Even if this were not so, 'this is not the way truth ought to be held by a rational being. Truth, thus held, is but one superstition the more, accidentally clinging to the words which enunciate a truth.' (76, pp.95-6) Expedience and morality both push in the same direction.

Marxist attacks on productivity deals
Despite his reluctance to put manipulation in a separate category from authority Fox is still very concerned that subordinates' consent should be based on 'the fullest information possible'. Without this firm foundation to consent pluralism is in danger of becoming an ideologically tainted celebration of the existing social order, a covert defence of existing inequalities of wealth, influence and power by the operation of which consent is often engineered. Pluralists have tended to be naive about the operation of power, concentrating their attention on obvious overt conflicts and ignoring the way in which power-holders can suppress incipient issues (often through simply doing nothing, the strategy of immobilism) and the methods that can be used to control people without the controlled being aware of it. (63, pp.11-15) On applying the crude equation of absence of overt conflict with absence of power, pluralists are likely to fail to detect the use of power where more incisive analyses would unmask it. The reliance of industrial relations pluralists on

social contract theory may simply reinforce this naivety because, as Lukes notes, the individualist notion of consent to government has itself been insensitive to the means by which power-holders can create and maintain the government's legitimacy. (62, pp.86-7)

It is no shock, then, that pluralists have come under fire from radicals, including Marxists. Marxists have emphasized the processes by which the ruling class develops an ideology cloaking social realities and passing off as eternal and unavoidable inequalities and injustices that are simply a product of the capitalist system and that will vanish after its overthrow. The totality of the socialization experiences of workers under capitalism produces an unenlightened acceptance of the existing social system. Marx wrote that 'the advance of capitalist production develops a working class which by education, tradition, habit, looks upon the conditions of that mode of production as self-evident laws of nature . . . the dull compulsion of economic relations completes the subjection of the labourer to the capitalist'. (75, pp. 261-4) When these selfsame workers engage in productivity bargaining they do so as men and women whose social outlook and aspirations have been moulded by a system that supports not their interests but those of the owners of the means of production.

While pluralists have been calling for a revolution in the attitudes of managers Marxists have been set on consciousness-raising activities of their own: alerting workers to the dangers of productivity bargaining so that any 'consent' will be properly informed. Cliff's book on the fight against productivity deals is a leading example of this genre. For Cliff, productivity bargaining signifies a determined onslaught by employers to regain some of the power they have lost in the post-war era. Workers have to be warned of the grave risks they run in listening to the blandishments of 'progressive' employers. Suspect, too, are the unions themselves. Full-time trade union officials as Cliff portrays them are a highly paid, caste-like bureaucracy, decked with the trappings of the middle class, often seeing themselves as members of the middle class, and increasingly cut off from the day-to-day and the long-term interests of those they claim to represent. Their avowed concern to uphold 'order' betrays their too close alignment with management. Their position in the power structure has been consolidated by the decline of branch activities, of district committees and trade councils, and also by the check-off system, where employers deduct union dues from the wages of employees and pay them directly to the union. (20, p.173ff) A key aim of productivity bargaining is to reduce the shop steward to the impotence of the full-time official, divorce him from his constituents, incorporate him into a rigid bureaucratic machine and shear him of his independent power and his militancy. Although he admits that there is evidence that shop stewards are not typically more militant than the men they serve Cliff argues that this is not the whole story. He says that if stewards lose their militancy we will see the growth of 'unofficial unofficial strikes' — ones without even the blessing of shop stewards. In addition he follows McCarthy and Parker in saying that stewards *are* somewhat more advanced than their constituents, as shown by their more frequent attendance at branch meetings and their greater propensity to pay the political levy to the Labour Party. (They are also more likely to be members of the Communist Party than are ordinary trade unionists, but Cliff does not mention this, probably feeling that it is a sign of reaction rather than militancy.) The evidence of their militancy that Cliff refers to might well be considered thin; certainly, McCarthy and Parker themselves make little of it. Nevertheless, despite the limited, defensive, fragmentary character of shop steward activities they are, says Cliff, a true expression of the urge to control, 'the embryo of full working-class control at every level of society, political and economic alike'. (20, p.203) Enlightened stewards will lead the resistance to productivity deals. They will see that productivity bargaining, with its goal of introducing 'order' into industry through the formulation of agreed procedural and substantive rules, is simply an expression of the urge felt by pluralists to 'institutionalize' industrial conflict, that is, to contain it closely so that it will not spill over into class conflict threatening the fabric of capitalist society. The proletarian who consents to the institutionalization of industrial relations is suffering from 'false consciousness'.

Interests and false consciousness

Is the pluralist powerless against this kind of criticism from the Left? Is pluralism doomed to be a sophisticated defence of what exists? Does pluralism by its very nature deny itself the concept of false consciousness, thereby ignoring one facet of the working of power in society? — Many people would say 'Yes' to these questions. Balbus, for example, compares pluralism unfavourably with Marxism exactly on these grounds. His analysis focusses on the interpretations pluralists and Marxists give to the concept of 'interests'. Pluralists, according to him, refuse to allow for the existence of objective individual and class interests and therefore cannot examine false consciousness at all. They argue that interests are always subjective: interests are nothing more than wants. To them it makes no sense to say that something is in someone's objective interests even though he does not want it; for his interests *are* his wants. This equation applies not only to individuals but also to social groups. In contrast to this stands the Marxist analysis. By giving prominence to objective interests, says Balbus, the Marxist account has analytical and normative advantages over its anaemic pluralist rival. First, it reflects the richness of our everyday language, in which interests are not simply equated with wants. Second, it enables us to examine the way in which desires are themselves socially generated and socially suppressed. Instead of ignoring the derivation of wants — as liberal economists do when they take the individual's 'utility function' as given — Marxists recognize that 'an individual's subjective interests are not merely *given,* or *randomly* generated, but rather are systematically determined by the way in which his life-chances are objectively affected by objective conditions'. (2, p.153) Marx himself was keen to specify the factors that favoured the growth of a class 'in itself' into a class 'for itself', that is, the conditions under which social classes, becoming aware of their shared objective class interests, develop a revolutionary class consciousness and an awareness of the contradiction or irreconcilability of their own interests with those of antagonistic social classes in the capitalist system. Conversely, Marx examined the factors that created false consciousness and hampered the growth of classes for themselves. Finally, say Balbus, the concept of objective interests provides a meeting-point for statements of fact and judgements of value. By discovering the objective interests of an individual or class we arm ourselves with a means of assessing the merits of any policy, political regime or social order.

For all its ready appeal Balbus's argument trivializes the pluralist position and obscures the Marxist one. For the critical difference between pluralists and Marxists rests not on the distinction between subjective and objective interests but on that between interest as a want-regarding and interest as an ideal-regarding concept, to use Barry's terms. Want-regarding principles are ones 'which take as given the wants which people happen to have and concentrate attention entirely on the extent to which a certain policy will alter the overall amount of want-satisfaction or on the way in which the policy will affect the distribution among people of opportunities for satisfying them . . . In order to evaluate the desirability of a state of affairs according to such principles, all the information we need is the amount and/or distribution among persons of want-satisfaction.' (3, p.38) This does not, however, exclude the possibility of distinguishing best from expressed interests. A man acting against his best interests is one who by following his present desires is in danger of jeopardizing, through ignorance or lack of foresight, *desires that he will probably have in the future or conflicting desires that he already has.* Barry writes: 'The contrast is not between want-satisfaction and something other than want-satisfaction, but rather between want-satisfaction now and want-satisfaction later . . . Want-satisfaction must be considered as a flow over time and at a certain point one is entitled to decide that someone who satisfies his present want is going to reduce his chances of satisfying future wants to an unreasonable degree.' (3, pp.185-6) To this must be added, as indicated above, the remark that an individual may have failed to realize that even his *present* desires clash, and that by pursuing one of them he may be frustrating other, more salient desires.

Plamenatz admits too that we can speak of an individual's best as opposed to perceived interests provided that we do not depart from interest as a want-regarding concept. When we say that something is not in an individual's best interests we are, says Plamenatz, predicting his future wants: if his present desires were met he would not like the consequences. We are emphatically not offering a moral judgement of his wants, present or future. Instead, we are considering the possibility that some of his present wants may have unforseen and undesired results. In making this kind of judgement we rely on what we know of the individual's tastes and of his probable future. (80, pp.316-8)

For Marxists, objective interests are not defined in relation to wants at all. Instead, they rest upon an ideal — a conception of the nature of man in society and of the historical process of the progressive realization of man's full potential. Social classes are the prime agents of social change, and a class is said to suffer from false consciousness if it fails to see and act out its historical mission. The Marxist does not tell us how to fulfil the desires we already have without jeopardizing other desires we have or may have in the future. He tells us what desires we *ought* to have. That is what he means by our objective interests; and false consciousness consists precisely in our adherence to 'false' goals and profession of 'false' needs. The falsity is a quality that can be determined objectively and irrefragably by Marxist analysis. Whereas pluralists, in the liberal tradition, act as midwives to desire, Marxists gladly practice abortion.

Balbus is correct in arguing, however, that many pluralists have refused to speak of false consciousness. They assert that their liberal values prevent them from doing more than taking other people's wants as given and equating those wants with interests. These are the same reasons some pluralists would give for not worrying whether or not workers' consent to productivity deals is, in Fox's terms, 'fully informed'. What I am arguing is that pluralists *can* examine the ways in which wants are socially generated and *can* use the concept of false consciousness. They can do these things *without abandoning their liberal values,* as Barry, Plamenatz and others have shown. What is more, liberalism's supreme concern to uphold liberty *requires* pluralists to take their analysis in these directions. For if we must be prepared to interpret an individual's best interests in the light of his future wants then equally we should examine the extent to which past wants have been modified or even abandoned in the face of obstacles to their fulfilment. Liberty is more than the absence of obstacles to a person's current desires: if it were only this it would be possible to increase one's freedom by abandoning frustrated wants or by redefining those wants. (7, p. xxxviii) Processes such as these do occur, and the sociologist has to be sensitive to them. An apt illustration is provided by Chinoy's classic, *Automobile Workers and the American Dream*. (17) Chinoy argues that manual workers in the United States, called upon to pursue advancement and success in a land where opportunities are equally available to all, find that the facts of their situation mean that chances are severely limited. The rhetoric of equal opportunity persuades many of them that 'failure' is due only to personal shortcomings, mainly to laziness. Now, Chinoy's car workers were not living up to the American Dream. They were not launched on a career in which they could reasonably expect a gradual progression to more skilled, desirable and better paid jobs; recruitment to higher positions in the company was biased more and more to well-qualified outsiders rather than to long-serving men from the factory floor; and the fragmented and routinized nature of their work made it hard for them to display their skills. The result was that within the company they had to work for collective improvement in wages and conditions instead of individual advancement. Hopes of getting on outside the company were largely confined to high-risk low-profit ventures the capital investment for which they found it hard to stump up owing to the difficulty they had in saving or borrowing money. Caught in a conflict between dream and actuality the car workers reacted *by redefining success*. This they did by enlarging the meaning of ambition to take in the quest for job security and small concessions from the firm; by taking pride in the accumulation of personal possessions; and by striving vicariously for success through their children.

If the liberal is interested not simply in a person's wants at a given time but also in the way in which those wants came about, then he should be concerned with the shaping and modification of aspirations in the light of experience. Although Chinoy found that his sample of car workers had high aspirations for their children most sociologists have found, to the contrary, that working-class parents have lower aspirations for their children's educational and occupational careers than do middle-class parents. Findings of this kind have been repeated time and again, with the upshot that a low level of aspiration is often taken to be characteristic of working-class subcultures. When the team conducting the 'Affluent Worker' research found that their sample of working-class parents had surprisingly high aspirations for their children this was not thought to be a refutation of the existing literature on the subject so much as an example of the difference in outlook of affluent workers in Luton from that of 'solidaristic', 'traditional' workers. But despite this similarity to typically middle-class patterns of aspiration certain working-class features remained: the affluent workers did not discuss their children's work so frequently, felt themselves less able to help with school work, were more hesitant and unsure in their dealings with the school and were less aware of the different opportunities offered by various forms of schooling and of the educational qualifications needed for particular jobs. Most significantly, it appeared that the actual performance of children who had already entered secondary school or the job market was far behind the general level of parental aspirations. (42, pp.129-140) It is likely, I would argue, that as the children failed to live up to the aspirations held for them the aspirations would be revised downwards and the original hopes forgotten or repressed. We know, after all, that much the same happens to children's own occupational and educational aspirations. It has been shown many times that children who fail qualifying examinations or who are put into the lower streams of a school quite quickly lower their expectations in comparison with those of their former classmates. Thus Liversidge's investigation of a small number of Primary, Secondary Modern and Grammar Schools in Leicestershire showed that 'pupils are fully aware of the social implications of their educational selection'. (58, p.23) Entrance to a Grammar School had an elevating effect and entrance to a Secondary Modern School a depressing effect on pupils' job aspirations. Liversidge adds that these aspirations were strikingly 'realistic', that is, in line with the actual structure of opportunities awaiting them.

Suppose we accept the accumulated evidence that school-children have very 'realistic' expectations of employment, and that although they often have 'fantasy' wishes they recognize them as fantasy and rarely confuse them with their quite separate realistic expectations. Add to this the argument that they and their parents may start with extremely high hopes and scale them down as they learn — from schoolteachers' advice and reports, examination results, processes of selection, and the experience of others — that their expectations are 'too high'. Ought we to regard this state of affairs as a mark of the commonsense, rationality and resistance to adolescent fantasy of the nation's youth? Ought we to say that the fact that parents and children adopt realistic expectations is socially functional, since it means that society is not creating expectations that cannot be fulfilled? Or should we say that the limited, fatalistic subculture of the working class is the outcome of a social system in which subordinate groups are denied freedom of choice without their being fully aware of the unfreedom?

For too long students of industrial relations have felt themselves able to ignore questions of this kind. It seems quite likely that in so far as they do respond to Fox's critique of pluralism and his call for 'full information' they will emphasize the demand that firms should 'open the books'. Workers and their representatives should have as much information as possible about the financial position of the firm and the industry. Employers should be willing to reveal more than they do at present, and unions will have to rouse themselves. On this last point it is unencouraging to learn that trade unions showed little interest in the recent Sandilands inquiry into methods of company accounting. The reason the unions gave was that this was a 'technical' question.

When Fox talks of 'full information' he means more than this, including knowledge 'not only about the great disparity of power in society but more especially about the conventional assumptions relating to authority, hierarchy, privileges and rewards'. (34, p.224) What he wants is a more open, self-questioning society in which social institutions and values are examined and discussed openly and frankly. Fine tuning of the institutions of industrial relations will not accomplish such a task by itself.

Productivity bargaining as conceived by its pluralist advocates is more than an economic gadget to lift firms' profit position and prospects for growth, to improve the wages and conditions of work of labour or to play an integral part in national economic policy. Productivity bargaining also expresses a thoroughgoing change in the relations between managers and managed. Basing their case on a social contract theory of government pluralists argue that the legitimacy of managerial rule is conferred by the active consent of workers. Workers are seen as predominantly rational beings who have an appreciable amount of power and who have developed ever higher aspirations under full employment and during a period of economic growth. In this situation, to put it bluntly, coercion and manipulation will not work for long, quite apart from any moral considerations that may rule them out. What is called for, on the grounds of morality and of prudence, is the greater incorporation of workers into the decision-making process. This will require a change not only in the structure of collective bargaining but also in attitudes on both sides of industry. Workers' consent must be sought to so-called 'market' relations, to rates of pay and conditions of work; but as well as this, so the argument runs, workers have a legitimate role to play in deciding how resources, including their own labour power, are to be deployed and used. These decisions, traditionally the prerogative of management, have to be shared.

A serious weakness of much of the literature on industrial relations in Great Britain is that it overlooks or treats too lightly the social and economic environment in which the business of collective bargaining is carried out. The weakness shows itself in many ways. For example, the economic problems that productivity bargaining in one enterprise can cause for other firms is given very summary treatment in Flanders' book on Fawley. Again, there is a lack of interest in the problem of the allocation of resources in the economy as a whole and an undue briskness towards questions of social justice — for why should increased productivity mean higher benefits? More important for the theme of this book is that in emphasizing the need to gain workers' consent pluralists have been slow to take an interest in the social sources of that consent. Pluralists have wanted to distinguish consent from acquiescence; but are we speaking of the consent of properly informed citizens or the consent of the ignorant and the duped? Are we considering a genuine attempt to raise levels of social consciousness in our society and to extend democratic processes from the ballot box to the factory floor, or are we dealing with what will prove to be confidence tricks in aid of current patterns of inequality and current definitions of appropriate behaviour?

Industrial relations pluralists must face up to these questions. To do so they will need to broaden their outlook by paying more attention to relevant work done by other social scientists and by taking seriously the injunction that systems of industrial relations be seen as embedded in a wider social framework. In both these respects the Webbs set a fine example.

Bibliography

1. E. W. Bakke, C. Kerr, C. W. Anrod (eds.), *Unions, Management and the Public* (2nd. edn.). New York, Harcourt Brace, 1960.

2. Isaac D. Balbus, 'The Concept of Interest in Pluralist and Marxian Analysis'. *Politics and Society*, 1, 2, 1971, 151-177.

3. B. M. Barry, *Political Argument*. London, Routledge, 1965.

4. H. S. Becker, *Sociological Work*. London, Allen Lane, 1971.

5. Hilde Behrend, 'The Effort Bargain'. *Industrial and Labour Relations Review*, 10, 4, 1957, 503-515.

6. R. Bendix, *Work and Authority in Industry*. New York, Wiley, 1956.

7. Isaiah Berlin, *Four Essays on Liberty*. London, OUP, 1969.

8. H. Beynon & R. M. Blackburn, *Perceptions of Work*. Cambridge, CUP, 1972.

9. H. Beynon, *Working for Ford*. Harmondsworth, Penguin, 1973.

10. R. K. Brown & P. Brannen, 'Social Relations and Social Perspectives amongst Shipbuilding Workers — a Preliminary Statement'. *Sociology*, 4, 1, 1970, 71-84, & 4, 2, 1970, 197-211.

11. W. A. Brown, *Piecework Bargaining*. London, Heinemann, 1973.

12. W. Buckley, *Sociology and Modern Systems Theory*.

Englewood Cliffs, Prentice-Hall, 1967.

13. Cameron, *Report of a Court of Inquiry into the Problems Caused by the Introduction of Web-Offset Machines in the Printing Industry.* London, HMSO, 1967, Cmnd. 3184.

14. I. C. Cannon, 'Ideology and Occupational Community: a Study of Compositors'. *Sociology,* 1, 2, 1967, 165-185.

15. M. K. Chandler, *Management Rights and Union Interests.* New York, McGraw-Hill, 1964.

16. J. Child, *Industrial Relations in the British Printing Industry.* London, Allen & Unwin, 1967.

17. E. Chinoy, *Automobile Workers and the American Dream.* New York, Doubleday, 1955.

18. H. A. Clegg, *A New Approach to Industrial Democracy.* Oxford, Blackwell, 1960.

19. H. A. Clegg, *The System of Industrial Relations in Great Britain.* Oxford, Blackwell, 1970.

20. Tony Cliff, *The Employers' Offensive: Productivity Deals and How to Fight Them.* London, Pluto Press, 1970.

21. Department of Employment, *The Reform of Collective Bargaining at Plant and Company Level* (Manpower Papers no. 5). London, HMSO, 1971.

22. Devlin, *Final Report of the Committee of Inquiry under the Rt. Hon. Lord Devlin into Certain Matters Concerning the Port Transport Industry.* London, HMSO, 1965, Cmnd. 2734.

23. A. V. Dicey, *Lectures on the Relation between Law and Public Opinion in England during the Nineteenth Century.* London, Macmillan, 1914.

24. Donovan, *Report, Royal Commission on Trade Unions and Employers' Associations, 1965-1968.* London, HMSO, 1968, Cmnd. 3623.

25. Donovan Secretariat, *Research Paper Four (Productivity Bargaining; Restrictive Labour Practices), Royal Commission on Trade Unions and Employers' Associations.* London, HMSO, 1967.

26. Engineering Employers' Federation, *Minutes of Evidence (no. 20) to the Royal Commission on Trade Unions and Employers' Associations.* London, HMSO, 1966.

27. Engineering Employers' Federation, *Written Evidence to the Royal Commission on Trade Unions and Employers' Associations.* No date.

28. Esso Petroleum Co. Ltd., *Minutes of Evidence (no. 39) to the Royal Commission on Trade Unions and Employers' Associations.* London, HMSO, 1966.

29. E. E. Evans-Pritchard, *Witchcraft, Oracles and Magic among the Azande.* Oxford, OUP, 1937.

30. Allan Flanders, *The Fawley Productivity Agreements.* London, Faber, 1964.

31. Allan Flanders, 'Collective Bargaining: a Theoretical Analysis'. *British Journal of Industrial Relations,* 6, 1, 1968, 1-26.

32. Alan Fox, 'Labour Utilization and Industrial Relations', pp.41-64 of D. Pym, (ed.), *Industrial Society: Social Sciences in Management.* Harmondsworth, Penguin, 1968.

33. Alan Fox, *A Sociology of Work in Industry.* London, Collier-Macmillan, 1971.

34. Alan Fox, 'Industrial Relations: a Social Critique of Pluralist Ideology', pp.185-233 of J. Child, (ed.), *Man and Organization.* London, Allen & Unwin, 1973.

35. Alan Fox & Allan Flanders, 'The Reform of Collective Bargaining: from Donovan to Durkheim'. *British Journal of Industrial Relations,* 7, 2, 1969, 151-180.

36. W. Friedmann, *Law in a Changing Society.* Harmondsworth, Penguin, 1964.

37. J. H. Goldthorpe, 'Vilfredo Pareto', pp.110-118 of T. Raison (ed.), *The Founding Fathers of Social Science.* Harmondsworth, Penguin, 1969.

38. J. H. Goldthorpe, 'Social Inequality and Social Integration in Modern Britain'. *Advancement of Science,* Dec. 1969, 190-202.

39. J. H. Goldthorpe, 'Class, Status and Party in Modern Britain'. *Archives Européennes de Sociologie,* 13, 2, 1972, 342-372.

40. J. H. Goldthorpe, 'Industrial Relations in Great Britain: a Critique of Reformism'. *Politics & Society,* 4, 4, 1974, 419-452.

41. J. H. Goldthorpe, D. Lockwood, F. Bechhofer, J. Platt, *The Affluent Worker: Industrial Attitudes and Behaviour.* Cambridge, CUP, 1968.

42. J. H. Goldthorpe, D. Lockwood, F. Bechhofer, J. Platt, *The Affluent Worker in the Class Structure.* Cambridge,

CUP, 1969.

43. W. Gomberg, 'The Work Rules and Work Practices Problem', pp. 109-121 of P. A. Weinstein, (ed.), *Featherbedding and Technological Change*. Boston, Heath, 1965.

44. P. T. Hartman, *Collective Bargaining and Productivity: the Longshore Mechanization Agreement*.

45. C. G. Hempel, *Aspects of Scientific Explanation*. New York, Free Press, 1965.

46. L. J. Henderson, *On the Social System* (ed. B. Barber). Chicago, Chicago UP, 1970.

47. D. J. Hickson & M. W. Thomas, 'Professionalization in Britain: a Preliminary Measurement'. *Sociology*, 3, 1, 1969, 37-53.

48. E. J. Hobsbawm, *Labouring Men*. London, Weidenfeld & Nicolson, 1964.

49. E. C. Hughes, *The Sociological Eye*. Chicago, Aldine-Atherton, 1971.

50. L. C. Hunter, G. L. Reid, D. Boddy, *Labour Problems of Technological Change*. London, Allen & Unwin, 1970.

51. *International Labour Review*, 82, 1, 1960, 59-69, 'Labour Dispute and Settlement in the United States Steel Industry'.

52. International Publishing Corporation, *Minutes of Evidence (no. 59) to the Royal Commission on Trade Unions and Employers' Associations*. London, HMSO, 1966.

53. T. J. Johnson, *Professions and Power*. London, Macmillan, 1972.

54. C. C. Killingsworth, 'The Modernization of West Coast Longshore Work Rules'. *Industrial and Labour Relations Review*, 15, 1962, 295-306.

55. M. D. King, 'Science and the Professional Dilemma', pp. 35-73 of J. Gould (ed.), *Penguin Social Sciences Survey, 1968*. Harmondsworth, Penguin, 1968.

56. J. W. Kuhn, *Bargaining in Grievance Settlement*. New York, Columbia University Press, 1961.

57. D. S. Lees, *The Economic Consequences of the Professions*. London, Institute of Economic Affairs, 1966.

58. W. Liversidge, 'Life Chances'. *Sociological Review*, 10, 1, 1962, 17-34.

59. John Locke, *The Second Treatise of Civil Government and*

A Letter Concerning Toleration (ed. J. W. Gough). Oxford, Blackwell, 1946.

60. D. Lockwood, *The Blackcoated Worker*. London, Allen & Unwin, 1958.

61. D. Lockwood, 'Sources of Variation in Working-Class Images of Society'. *Sociological Review*, 14, 3, 1966, 249-267.

62. S. Lukes, *Individualism*. Oxford, Blackwell, 1973.

63. S. Lukes, *Power: a Radical View*. London, Macmillan, 1974.

64. T. Lupton, *On the Shop Floor*. Oxford, Pergamon, 1963.

65. W. E. J. McCarthy, *The Closed Shop in Britain*. Oxford, Blackwell, 1964.

66. W. E. J. McCarthy, *The Role of Shop Stewards in British Industrial Relations*. Research Paper 1, Royal Commission on Trade Unions and Employers' Associations. London, HMSO, 1966.

67. W. E. J. McCarthy & S. R. Parker, *Shop Stewards and Workshop Relations*. Research Paper 10, Royal Commission on Trade Unions and Employers' Associations. London, HMSO, 1968.

68. W. E. J. McCarthy & N. D. Ellis, *Management by Agreement*. London, Hutchinson, 1973.

69. Henry Sumner Maine, *Ancient Law*. London, OUP, 1959.

70. A. I. Marsh, *Industrial Relations in Engineering*. Oxford, Pergamon, 1965.

71. A. I Marsh, E. O. Evans, P. Garcia, *Workplace Industrial Relations in Engineering*. London, Kogan Page, 1971.

72. Elton Mayo, *The Human Problems of an Industrial Civilization*. Cambridge (Mass.), Harvard UP, 1946.

73. M. Mellish, *The Docks after Devlin*. London, Heinemann, 1972.

74. R. Michels, *Political Parties*. New York, Free Press, 1962.

75. R. Miliband, *The State in Capitalist Society*. London, Weidenfeld & Nicolson, 1969.

76. John Stuart Mill, 'On Liberty', in *Utilitarianism, Liberty and Representative Government* (ed. A. D. Lindsay). London, Dent, 1962.

77. National Board for Prices and Incomes, *Report no. 36: Productivity Agreements*. London, HMSO, 1967, Cmnd. 3311.

132   Bibliography

78. H. R. Northrup, *Restrictive Labour Practices in the Supermarket Industry.* Philadelphia, University of Pennsylvania Press, 1967.

79. P. H. Partridge, *Consent and Consensus.* London, Pall Mall, 1971.

80. J. Plamenatz, *Man and Society, vol. 2.* London, Longman, 1963.

81. J. Rex, 'The Future of Race Relations Research in Britain: Sociological Research and the Politics of Racial Justice'. *Race,* 14, 4, 1973, 481-488.

82. F. J. Roethlisberger & W. J. Dickson, *Management and the Worker.* Cambridge (Mass.), Harvard University Press, 1939.

83. D. F. Roy, 'Efficiency and "The Fix",' pp. 359-379 of T. Burns (ed.), *Industrial Man.* Harmondsworth, Penguin, 1969.

84. G. P. Schultz & R. B. McKersie, 'Stimulating Productivity: Choices, Problems, and Shares'. *British Journal of Industrial Relations,* 5, 1, 1967, 1-18.

85. Shawcross, *Report, Royal Commission on the Press, 1961-1962.* London, HMSO, 1962, Cmnd. 1811.

86. H. A. Shepard, 'Responses to Situations of Competition and Conflict', pp. 127-137 of R. L. Kahn & E. Boulding (eds.), *Power and Conflict in Organizations.* London, Tavistock, 1964.

87. J. H. Skolnick, *Justice Without Trial.* New York, Wiley, 1966.

88. S. H. Slichter, J. J. Healy, E. R. Livernash, *The Impact of Collective Bargaining on Management.* Washington DC, Brookings Institution, 1960.

89. A. J. M. Sykes, 'Unity and Restrictive Practices in the British Printing Industry'. *Sociological Review,* 8, 1960, 239-254.

90. F. W. Taylor, *Shop Management.* New York, Harper, 1911.

91. F. W. Taylor, *The Principles of Scientific Management.* New York, Harper, 1914.

92. B. A. Turner, *Exploring the Industrial Subculture.* London, Macmillan, 1971.

93. C. Turner & M. N. Hodge, 'Occupations and Professions', chap. 2 of J. A. Jackson (ed.), *Professions and Professionalization*. Cambridge, CUP, 1970.

94. H. A. Turner, *Trade Union Growth, Structure and Policy*. London, Allen & Unwin, 1962.

95. H. A. Turner, 'The Royal Commission's Research Papers'. *British Journal of Industrial Relations*, 6, 3, 1968, 346-359.

96. H. A. Turner, G. Clack, G. Roberts, *Labour Relations in the Motor Industry*. London, Allen & Unwin, 1967.

97. R. E. Walton & R. B. McKersie, *A Behavioural Theory of Labour Negotiations*. New York, McGraw-Hill, 1965.

98. Sidney & Beatrice Webb, *Industrial Democracy*. London, Longmans, 1902.

99. Sidney & Beatrice Webb, *The History of Trade Unionism*. London, Longmans, 1907.

100. D. Wedderburn & R. Crompton, *Workers' Attitudes and Technology*. Cambridge, CUP, 1972.

101. P. A. Weinstein (ed.), *Featherbedding and Technological Change*. Boston, Heath, 1965.

102. W. F. Whyte, 'Human Relations — a Progress Report', pp. 100-112 of A. Etzioni (ed.), *Complex Organizations: a Sociological Reader*. New York, Holt, 1961.

103. H. L. Wilensky, 'The Professionalization of Everyone?'. *American Journal of Sociology*, 70, 2, 1964, 137-158.

104. D. F. Wilson, *Dockers*. London, Fontana, 1972.

105. F. Zweig, *Productivity and Trade Unions*. Oxford, Blackwell, 1951.

Index